The Case for Degrowth

T0056389

Giorgos Kallis
Susan Paulson
Giacomo D'Alisa
Federico Demaria

———

The Case for Degrowth

polity

Copyright © Giorgos Kallis, Susan Paulson, Giacomo D'Alisa, and Federico Demaria 2020

The right of Giorgos Kallis, Susan Paulson, Giacomo D'Alisa, and Federico Demaria to be identified as Authors of this Work has been asserted in accordance with the UK Copyright, Designs and Patents Act 1988.

First published in 2020 by Polity Press

Polity Press
65 Bridge Street
Cambridge CB2 1UR, UK

Polity Press
101 Station Landing
Suite 300
Medford, MA 02155, USA

All rights reserved. Except for the quotation of short passages for the purpose of criticism and review, no part of this publication may be reproduced, stored in a retrieval system or transmitted, in any form or by any means, electronic, mechanical, photocopying, recording or otherwise, without the prior permission of the publisher.

ISBN-13: 978-1-5095-3562-0
ISBN-13: 978-1-5095-3563-7 (pb)

A catalogue record for this book is available from the British Library.

Library of Congress Cataloging-in-Publication Data

Names: Kallis, Giorgos, author.
Title: The case for degrowth / Giorgos Kallis, Susan Paulson, Giacomo D'Alisa, and Federico Demaria.
Description: Cambridge, UK ; Medford, MA : Polity Press, 2020. | Series: The case for series | Includes bibliographical references and index. | Summary: "A radical counterpoint to the 'growth at all costs' agenda"-- Provided by publisher.
Identifiers: LCCN 2020015130 (print) | LCCN 2020015131 (ebook) | ISBN 9781509535620 (hardback) | ISBN 9781509535637 (paperback) | ISBN 9781509535644 (epub)
Subjects: LCSH: Economic development. | Stagnation (Economics) | Poverty. | Sustainable development.
Classification: LCC HD75 .K35 2020 (print) | LCC HD75 (ebook) | DDC 338.9--dc23
LC record available at https://lccn.loc.gov/2020015130
LC ebook record available at https://lccn.loc.gov/2020015131

Typeset in 11 on 15 Sabon by Servis Filmsetting Ltd, Stockport, Cheshire
Printed and bound in the UK by TJ International Limited

The publisher has used its best endeavours to ensure that the URLs for external websites referred to in this book are correct and active at the time of going to press. However, the publisher has no responsibility for the websites and can make no guarantee that a site will remain live or that the content is or will remain appropriate.

Every effort has been made to trace all copyright holders, but if any have been overlooked the publisher will be pleased to include any necessary credits in any subsequent reprint or edition.

For further information on Polity, visit our website: politybooks.com

Contents

Preface

As this book goes to press, in April 2020, the World Health Organization has declared a global pandemic of COVID-19. We write these lines quarantined in our homes in Barcelona and Florida. We are not prophets, so we cannot predict how health and economic crises will have unfolded by the time you read this book. One thing we do know is that the case for degrowth will remain as relevant as ever.

We make a case for attributing current ecological disequilibrium and a range of social ills to the relentless pursuit of growth. It would be naive to claim that this pandemic is proof of limits to growth, a messianic reckoning for our unsustainable ways. Epidemics happened in the past and will happen in the future. Yet the speed and scope of this contagion are clearly driven by interconnectivities of accelerated global economies, exemplified in its spread via airplane and ship routes. The growing ease with which viruses jump from animals to humans is conditioned by expansion of corporate agricultural systems, encroachment of humans on habitats, and the commodification of wildlife, all integral to current growth economies.

The failure of some leaders to respond quickly and to protect their populations, as well as urges to restart economies before the pandemic is over, can likewise be understood in the context of ongoing pushes to sustain growth analyzed in this book. One dangerous dimension of these pushes is rejection of scientific evidence and advice. In recent decades, climate change deniers have undermined faith in science among a portion of the public in efforts to defend fossil-fueled growth. Not welcoming scientific findings that threaten growth economies, some governments have cut funding for pandemic research units and epidemic control teams, as well as studies on mitigation and adaptation to climate change.

Several decades of budget cuts to public health and to social and civil security infrastructures, enacted in the name of economic growth, have eroded capacities of many states to respond to this crisis. The pandemic has lain bare the fragility of existing economic systems. Wealthy nations have more than enough resources to cover public health and basic needs during a crisis, and could weather declines in non-essential parts of the economy by reallocating work and resources to essential ones. Yet the way current economic systems are organized around constant circulation, any decline in market activity threatens systemic collapse, provoking generalized unemployment and impoverishment. It doesn't have to be this way. To be more resilient to future crises – pandemic, climatic, financial, or political – we need to build systems capable of scaling back production in ways that do not cause loss of livelihood or life.

Some of you might protest, "Isn't the coronavirus crisis revealing the misery of degrowth?" We invite you to first read this book. What is happening during the pandemic is *not* degrowth. The goal of degrowth is to purposefully slow things down in order to minimize harm to humans and earth systems. The current situation is terrible, not because carbon emissions are declining, which is good, but because many lives are lost; it is terrible not because GDPs are going down, to which we are indifferent, but because there are no processes in place to protect livelihoods when growth falters. For us, caring and community solidarity are vital principles of degrowth societies, and engines for moving in more equitable and sustainable directions.

We would like to see societies become slower by design, not disaster. This pandemic exemplifies the types of growth-induced disasters we diagnose in this book. The economic policies and social arrangements we propose offer ways to make such situations more livable and just, to emerge stronger and better post-crisis, and to reorient practices and politics that are setting the scene for future disasters.

The end of growth will not necessarily involve a smooth transition. It may very well be unplanned, unwilled, and messy, in conditions not of our own choosing. Conditions like the ones we are living through now. History often evolves with punctuations; our analysis shows how periods of paralysis can reach a tipping point, when unexpected events open new possibilities and violently close others. The COVID-19 pandemic is such an event. Suddenly, things take radical new directions, and the unthinkable becomes thinkable, for better or for worse. Severe economic depression led to Roosevelt's New Deal, and also to Hitler's Third Reich. What are the possibilities and dangers now?

Amid this pandemic, many scientific, political, and moral authorities are communicating the message that caring for people's health and wellbeing should come before profit, and that is great. A resurgence of the care ethic that we advocate is evident in the willingness of younger people to stay home to protect their elders, and in the spirit of duty and sacrifice among care and health workers. Of course, many stay home also because they fear the virus and worry about themselves, or to avoid police fines. And many care workers go to work because they must earn a living. But, as we argue, acting collectively against such crises requires combinations of sacrifice and solidarity, self and collective interest, government interventions and popular consensus about the right thing to do.

Deep inequalities are coming into play in new ways. While some have the luxury of sheltering at home, others must choose between unemployment without an adequate safety net and exposure to the coronavirus in jobs involving care work and provisioning. As the pandemic plays out differently in different parts of the world, those who are in more vulnerable identities and positions are likely to suffer more than others. These injustices coexist with an awareness that, unless whole populations are protected, not even the wealthiest are fully safe from contagion.

In this crisis, like others before, people have mobilized and self-organized where businesses and governments have failed to provide for their needs – from mutual aid groups delivering food and medicines for elders, to groups of doctors, engineers, and hackers collaborating to 3-D print components for oxygen ventilators, to students babysitting the children of doctors and nurses. The proliferation of caring and commoning endeavors, which form the bedrock of the degrowth societies we envision, are all the more commendable given the contagious nature of the virus. After the pandemic is over, and the difficult path of economic reconstruction starts, this resurgent dynamism of commoning and care will be vital.

Positive impulses among individuals and grassroots networks are necessary but not sufficient for sustained change. We need states to secure safety and healthcare, protect the environment, and provide economic safety nets. The policies we advocate in this book were necessary before the pandemic, and are vital during and after: a Green New Deal and public investment program, work-sharing, a basic care income, universal public services, and support of community economies. So is the reorganization of public finance through measures including carbon fees and taxes on wealth, high incomes, natural resource use, and pollution. Whereas our book focuses on demobilizing resource-intensive and ecologically damaging aspects of current economies, pandemic responses deal with demobilizing those aspects not immediately essential for sustaining life. We coincide in facing the fundamental challenge of managing political economies without growth during and after the pandemic: how to demobilize parts of the capitalist economy while securing the provisioning of basic goods and services, experimenting with resource-light ways of enjoying ourselves, and finding positive meanings in life.

Radical proposals are already being considered and selectively adopted across the political spectrum as they provide concrete solutions amid the pandemic. Companies and governments have reduced working hours and implemented work-sharing; different forms of basic income are being debated; financial measures have been instituted to subsidize workers in the quarantine period and after businesses close; an international campaign for care income has been launched; governments have engaged the productive apparatus to secure vital supplies and services; and moratoriums are being considered or imposed on rent, mortgage, and debt payments. There is growing understanding that vast government spending will be required.

Our book suggests ways we can reconstruct economies with the goal of mitigating crises that loom on the horizon, including a wide array of threats associated with climate change. This goal will not be met by subsidizing fossil fuel companies, airlines, cruise ships, and tourism mega-businesses. Instead, states need to finance Green New Deals and rebuild their health and care infrastructures, creating jobs in a just transition to economies that are less environmentally damaging. As oil prices fall, fossil fuels should be taxed heavily, raising funds to support green and social investments, and to provide tax breaks and dividends to working people. Rather than using public money to bail out corporations and banks, we urge the establishment of basic care incomes that will help people and communities to reconstruct their lives and livelihoods.

The world will change after the virus, and there will be struggles over which paths to take. People will have to fight to direct change toward more equitable and resilient societies that have gentler impacts on humans and natural environments. Powerful actors will try to reconstitute status quo arrangements, and to shift costs to those with less power. It takes organizing and a confluence of alliances and circumstances to ensure that it won't be the environment and the workers who pay the bill, but those who profited most from the growth that preceded this disaster.

This crisis arguably opens up more dangers than it does possibilities. We worry about the politics of fear that the coronavirus pandemic engenders, the intensification of surveillance and control of peoples' movements, xenophobia and blame of others, as well as home isolation that curbs commoning and political organizing. Once measures such as curfews, quarantines, rule-by-decree, border controls, or election postponements are taken, they can become part of the arsenal of political possibility, opening dystopian horizons.

To counter these risks, this book motivates and guides us to re-found societies on the commons of mutual aid and care, orienting collective pursuits away from growth and toward wellbeing and equity. These are not just lofty aspirations; we identify everyday practices and concrete policies to start building the world we want today, together with political strategies to support synergy among these efforts in the construction of equitable and low-impact societies.

When we were writing this book, we knew we would have to work hard to convince readers of the case for degrowth. Our job may be somewhat easier now amid such tangible evidence that the current system is crumbling under its own weight. As we embark on the second major global economic crisis in a dozen years, perhaps some of us will be more willing to question the wisdom of producing and consuming more and more, just to keep the system going. The time is ripe for us to refocus on what really matters: not GDP, but the health and well-being of our people and our planet.

In a word, degrowth.

Acknowledgments

For years now, the four of us have been writing about the negative impacts and disastrous futures of economic growth, while urging moves toward healthier horizons. This is the first book we dedicate to alternative paths forward. An organized transition to degrowth will be politically difficult, but we believe that it is possible, and that living and working toward that transition is good in itself.

Writing this book is an act of care. Care for family, friends, and fellow citizens striving to contribute and find meaning in the face of historic challenges. Care for people and places around the world struggling to survive the burdens and damages of growth. And care for each other, as collaborators and co-authors.

As in any act of care, our efforts to produce this book ran up against limits and vulnerabilities of our individual positions – class, gender, disciplinary, cul-

Acknowledgments

tural, and other. Together we have worked toward new understandings and acceptance. Convinced that meaningful and rewarding journeys are rarely the easiest ones, we hope that this book motivates and empowers differently positioned readers on their own challenging paths.

Giorgos Kallis is an ICREA professor at ICTA-UAB, where he teaches ecological economics and political ecology. He has studied how water has been mobilized to fuel the growth of cities and has devoted recent years to arguing against the folly of green growth. Giorgos's latest work is a defense of the notion of limits.

Susan Paulson, based at the University of Florida, studies and teaches about gender, class, and eth-noracial systems interacting with bodies and environments. She has researched and taught in Latin America for thirty years, fifteen of those living in South America among low-income, low-impact communities. Susan is currently studying changing masculinities among men who perform painful and dangerous labor in extractive industries.

Giacomo D'Alisa is based at CES-UC in Coimbra, Portugal, where he researches commons and commoning, arguing that a society that prospers without growth must be based around the commons. Giacomo has written about conflicts over waste in his native Campania, and about political strategies for degrowth, warning against discourses of "emergency."

Federico Demaria is a Serra Hunter lecturer in ecological economics and political ecology at the University of Barcelona, part of the Environmental Justice Atlas team that studies and maps environmental conflicts around the world. Federico has lived and worked with waste-pickers in Delhi, studying how environmentalisms of the poor can inform a pluriverse of alternatives to development.

In the collaborative production of this book, each of us contributed theoretical perspectives, contents, and critiques. Giorgos took the lead in bringing these together, conceptualizing the book, laying out its arguments, and writing first drafts of the chapters. The text you have in your hands, however, is the product of Susan's labor, writing, and rewriting each passage. Her language, approach, and anthropologist's attention to historical, cultural, and geographical context marks our difference from previous publications on degrowth dominated by economistic or environmental arguments. Giacomo's philosophy of life and politics is responsible for rooting our argument in the commons, and for the political strategy that permeates our case, a strategy of building common senses slowly through

Acknowledgments

deep cultural changes that are embodied and practiced. Federico brought experiences of dialogue with allied movements, and conducted research in Barcelona used to illustrate our arguments.

It has not been easy to navigate among four histories of thought and action. We debated heatedly about ways to honor, connect with, critique, or condemn a variety of positions and paths. Our constructive struggles may prefigure wider debates and tensions that we aim to impel among readers.

The understandings expressed in this book have developed through engagement with overlapping networks of scientists and activists, including colleagues and students at ICTA-UAB, Research & Degrowth, the Center for Latin American Studies at the University of Florida, the Ecology and Society group at CES, and the Entitle and Political Ecology Networks, as well as the participants of the international degrowth conferences and summer schools.

Let us also acknowledge critics of degrowth, past and future. We are grateful to those who care deeply enough to raise sharp questions and critiques, and to impel the continual clarification and adaptation of our understandings and proposals.

We are grateful to our editors Louise Knight and Inès Boxman, who have been at the heart of this book project since its conceptualization, and

Acknowledgments

– together with anonymous reviewers – provided valuable insights. Thanks also to William Boose and Juanita Duque, who helped to manage bibliography and review drafts.

We acknowledge support from the Spanish government (COSMOS and María de Maeztu grants – Kallis; CSO2017-88212-R), the European Research Council (EnvJustice project – Demaria; GA695446), and the Portuguese Foundation for Science and Technology (D'Alisa; UID/SOC/50012/2019).

As co-authors, we take responsibility for all gaps, errors, and inconsistencies in this book, with the hope that our limitations will spark future efforts. We offer the book as an invitation to explore strategies for social-ecological transformation, starting with ways of seeing, being, and interrelating. And we invite you to engage, learn more, and contribute to the conversation.

1

A Case for Degrowth

The case for degrowth is a case for stopping the pursuit of growth and for reorienting lives and societies toward wellbeing. This book impels moves to build good lives for all, and shows how existing resources can be shared and invested differently to secure good living with less money, less exploitation, and less environmental degradation. Readers will be familiar with the environmental damages and with the forms of inequality and exploitation presented in this book. What is different here is that we link these troubling phenomena to the imperative of modern economies to grow, and argue that overcoming them means moving away from the relentless drive for more.

Neither the exploitation of humans and natural resources, nor the generation of emissions and other waste, can continue to increase without exacerbating planetary crises. In Europe and North America, from where we write, sustaining growth is no longer economically sound: its social, ecological, and personal costs exceed its benefits. This condition is camouflaged by mechanisms that conceal social and ecological costs, externalizing them from accounting records, and that displace damages toward other places and people, including future generations.

There is no doubt about the evidence. Harmful environmental and social consequences of growth have been rigorously documented throughout the past half-century.[1] Yet, the quantity of matter and energy used by human economies continues to increase by the minute, while governments and businesses continue to promote what Greta Thunberg, in her speech at the 2019 UN Climate Action Summit, called "fairy tales of eternal economic growth."

What is delaying a change of course? Certainly, privileged actors exercise sophisticated means to sustain growth systems in which they enjoy disproportionately large benefits and bear few burdens and risks. However, even if Elon Musk flew the wealthiest 1% off to Mars, a drive for growth would persist in many – although not all – places and persons, even some of those most exploited and degraded by growth economies. The capacity to change course is constrained by particular modes of knowing and being that have become intertwined with expanding colonial, capitalist, and fossil fuel economies.

Globalization of these modes has displaced cultural, biological, linguistic, technological, kinship, religious, and other forms of diversity that have been fundamental to adaptation and resilience throughout human history. As worldviews and social systems that evolved historically with growth are disseminated and empowered over others worldwide, diverse groups struggle to sustain or to forge different lifeways, while those at the core find it difficult to imagine alternatives.

Many committed people respond to today's crises not by questioning growth, but by proposing to make it green and inclusive. Rather than slow down, conservatives and progressives alike have been pushing to grow the pie bigger in order to finance green technologies and social benefits. Politicians across the spectrum have been subsidizing growth in order to avoid recessions, nominally protecting those most vulnerable to economic downturns.

During the mid-twentieth century, growing pies did correspond with expanding middle classes and greater income equality in numerous countries. Starting in the 1980s, however, phenomenal growth in national and global pies has been tied to an increasingly unequal distribution of wealth and income within and between countries.[2] Despite more than ten consecutive years of GDP growth in the US, the gap between the richest and poorest households is the largest it has been in fifty years.[3] In the same period, environmental damage caused by growing pies disproportionately harmed people who were already poor or marginalized, including millions who have become climate refugees. Growth has also fostered generational inequities by colonizing the future with legacies of debt, damage, and instability.

Yannis Varoufakis argues for qualitatively different growth: "we must end," he writes, "the growth of 'stuff' that is destroying the planet and people's life prospects (diesel cars, toxic farming, forest-leveling cattle farms, toxic finance) and promote the growth of the 'stuff' that humanity needs (green energy, care giving, education, sustainable housing)."[4] Surely we must do this. However, this book raises doubts about whether growth could be sustained by producing only good stuff, and whether such a shift would actually reduce environmental damage. Making good stuff still relies on making some bad stuff. Manufacture of solar panels, for example, requires extraction of rare minerals, destroying mountains and contaminating rivers; transportation of materials and panels by ships and trucks, generating emissions; construction of roads, ports, and factories, destroying landscapes. At current rates of 3 percent annual growth, the global economy will become eleven times larger by the end of this century, so even significant shifts toward cleaner production would still result in manifold increases in environmental impacts.

Degrowth makes the case that we have to produce and consume differently, and also less. That we have to share more and distribute more fairly, while the pie shrinks. To do so in ways that support pleasurable and meaningful lives in resilient societies and environments requires values and institutions that produce different kinds of persons and relations.

Purpose

The purpose of this book is to motivate and empower citizens, policy-makers, and activists to reorient livelihoods and politics around equitable wellbeing. We aim to stimulate thoughts and actions toward building such worlds not only by theorizing new understandings and imagining other pathways, but also by developing viable strategies to move forward now.

People are working in multiple ways to foster such moves, from experimenting with daily practices and community life to engineering alternative food and monetary systems. This book foregrounds opportunities for synergy among ongoing changes in institutions, technologies, relations, (re)production of lifeworlds, and other spheres.

Coevolutionary change emerges via dynamism within and influences among spheres. At a given time, certain features may appear invariable, interlocked with others in an immutable system. But transformative potential can be unleashed through disruptive, often unpredictable, events as well as positive recognition of already existing diversity, together with adaptation, innovation, and unintentional mutations. This means paying attention to, and supporting interaction among, dominant and non-dominant practices and visions, institutionalized and grassroots processes, long-enduring traditions and new experiments.

The world is on the verge of radical transformations as great as those experienced by early modern Europe with the forging of industrial capitalism, and as deep as those undergone by diverse actors and lifeways reinvented as the "third world" during the twentieth century. Degradation of ecosystems and earth systems is already provoking disasters for many people. Diseases and pandemics are disrupting economies and everyday life. Compounding impacts will doubtlessly lead to more serious disruption for more people in more places, further destabilizing economies. Political responses to these challenges are taking various forms: neo-extractivism (expanding extractive industries while limiting expatriation of profits in order to finance social programs), authoritarian nationalism (growth at all costs with social programs for native-born citizens, but excluding immigrants), neoliberal austerity (cuts to the many to sustain the wealth of the few), or authoritarian austerity (cuts to the many to fund armaments and policing to handle unrest). *The Case for Degrowth* calls on readers to respond differently to this looming historic shift, with policies and actions that work together to support modest living, enjoyed in solidarity, amid shared abundance.

The rest of this chapter introduces ideas key to our case. Chapter 2 examines rising costs of growth, and Chapter 3 shows how people are already living lives and (re)producing relationships and institutions not driven toward growth futures. Chapters 4 and 5 outline political strategies through which governments and civil societies can create the conditions that support and strengthen initiatives on various scales and in multiple spheres, thus encouraging synergistic coevolution away from growth.

Material and Economic Growth

This book distinguishes increases in market activity and in materials used by human economies from other kinds of growth. "Material growth" refers to the increase in the quantity of matter and energy transformed by human societies (e.g. trees cut down, coal burned, plants and animals eaten). Researchers measure transformed materials with methods including material flows analysis and ecological footprints, and link the recent acceleration of material growth to climate change, ocean acidification, biodiversity loss, diminishing fresh water, and other crises.[5]

Planetary scientists agree that curbing material growth is necessary to mitigate these undesired impacts.[6] Experts are joined by millions of others who resist expansions that they perceive as undermining their lives and worlds via deforestation, desertification, erosion, water and air pollution, desiccation of rivers and springs, depletion of game and fish stock, and more. Among these are communities destabilized by melting glaciers in Peru and rising seawaters in the Maldives,[7] by lead poisoning and water crisis in Flint Michigan,[8] and by death in Louisiana's cancer alley.[9]

In this book, the term "economic growth" refers to increase in the monetary value of goods and services exchanged in a given market, calculated in each country as its Gross Domestic Product (GDP). In contrast to the broad consensus that material growth is environmentally damaging, economic growth is widely embraced as beneficial and necessary. Around the world, scholars, politicians, and development professionals use GDP growth as a proxy for and a means to all kinds of desired changes, in spite of statistical analyses demonstrating that greater economic equality correlates much better than higher GDPs with desired outcomes including higher rates of longevity, literacy, equality, security, political participation, mental health, and happiness; or lower rates of incarceration, obesity, homicide, and suicide.[10]

Chapter 2 urges readers to question some of the purported benefits of growth, and to acknowledge its undesired outcomes. It shows how economic growth continues to depend on social and geographic inequalities that facilitate an unequal exchange of materials and energy. The chapter also demonstrates that economic growth has been inseparably linked to damaging material growth, and is likely to remain so in the future. Although certain production processes have become cleaner and more resource-efficient, country-wide and global economic growth remains tied to grow- ing ecological footprints. A recent comprehensive review concludes: "not only is there no empirical evidence supporting the existence of a decoupling of economic growth from environmental pressures on anywhere near the scale needed to deal with envi- ronmental breakdown, but also, and perhaps more importantly, such decoupling appears unlikely to happen in the future."[11]

Rhythms of Growth

We distinguish three rhythms of growth: cycli- cal, perpetual, and compound. Biological growth is cyclical. Seeds grow into trees, human infants grow into adults; at some point each organism stops growing, then dies and decays, while new organisms begin to grow. Life cycles of individual organisms are integral to larger systems – forests, families, cities – in which other factors interact with biology to shape varying courses of expansion and diminution. Unusual growth also occurs: multiplying cancer cells produce tumors, invasive plants and animals overrun others, viruses proliferate in hosts, contagions doubling every few days. Yet, these bursts eventually meet conditions that slow or halt growth: the cancer host dies, the transformed habitat becomes inhospitable, populations develop immunity against viruses.

The obvious axiom that nothing can grow indefinitely was disregarded in the twentieth century, when desire for perpetual growth became a guiding force in economic science, and across political ideologies. Companies, banks, economists, and governments developed operational strategies that depended on continually growing profits and GDPs. Cycles in which children grew up to replace their parents became trajectories in which each generation was expected to earn more and consume more. Participants in these processes came to perceive perpetual growth as natural and right.

But there is nothing natural in perpetual growth. Trees do not grow into the heavens, like Jack's beanstalk, and human embryos do not grow into giants. Some human communities have grown into cities and empires, expanding gross and per capita use of material and energy. In the long term, however, cyclical rises and falls have punctuated an equilibrium in which the total metabolism of human societies on earth increased little during the first 99 percent of human history. Archeological records show that innumerable human groups sustained themselves over millennia in a relatively steady state. Even in the present age, groups ranging from Andaman Islanders to !Kung San live with remarkably low societal metabolism.[12] Yet perpetual growth has become common sense to citizens socialized by mass media, museums, and history books that incite the thrill of exceptional expansion, as in Roman, Mayan, or Inca empires, while remaining silent on the far more common steady state.

Over the past century, the era of growth that dawned with European colonialism took an unprecedented turn as increases in global GDP, use of resources, and generation of waste and emissions accelerated at rates known as "compound." The fantastical rates of compound growth call for a legendary illustration. When a delighted King in India asked the inventor of chess what reward he wanted, the inventor demanded a modest-sounding payment: one grain of rice on the first square of the chessboard, two on the second, four on the third, doubling each time. On the sixty-fourth square, the king would have to put more than 18,000,000,000,000,000,000 (18 billion billions) grains of rice.

Versions differ on whether the inventor became an honored advisor or had his head smoothly chopped off. Today, that legendary inventor could be a high-ranking economist promoting 3 percent annual growth that doubles an economy every twenty-four years, quadruples it in forty-eight, growing sixteen-fold in a century. Economists today are not dealing with grains of rice, however, but with a global economy that already extracts 92 billion tons of materials annually.[13]

The astounding eruption of compound growth has provoked paradoxical responses. Many analysts proclaim the end of an historic era, as breached planetary limits, depletion of cheap resources, and concomitant conflicts destabilize growth systems beyond repair. In contrast, many zealous politicians and businesspeople hope and plan for compound growth to continue.

Common Sense

Perpetual growth and compound growth seem senseless on a finite planet, yet to many people they make common sense. Among sales representatives trying to sell more and more each year, academics trying to publish more articles, consumers buying ever-bigger televisions, and business owners plotting expansions, the assumption is rarely questioned that to live well means to make more and consume more.

"Common sense" is generally defined as the exercise of sound judgment. Here we explore the historical assemblage of knowledge, values, and assumptions that, embodied through socialization and practice, set the scene for certain judgments to be perceived as sound, and others unsound. Common senses often work to protect the status quo by making business-as-usual appear natural and logical. Ideologies that portray conventional beliefs as self-evident truths can make it unthinkable (unethical, unpatriotic) to ask critical questions.

One silver lining of historical crises is their potential to destabilize established truths, opening transformative possibilities. Unsettled times often shift the ways we draw on coexisting realms of common sense. In the face of current challenges, for example, decision-making may bring to the surface tensions between common senses of individual achievement, rivalry, and domination cultivated in the marketplace and competing common senses of modesty, charity, and compassion long established in Christian teachings, as highlighted in Pope Francis's encyclical *On Care for Our Common Home*.[14]

A Case for Degrowth

In these turbulent times, how can we shine a light through the cracks in common senses of growth? How can we challenge judgments that justify pushing for perpetual growth, or getting ahead of one's neighbors?

Degrowth seeks to unsettle the common conviction that growth behavior is driven by natural instincts. Powerful cultural and scientific narratives portray evolution as driving humans toward economic expansion: "Humans are genetically programmed to always want more." "Growth results naturally when people are free to invent things that other people want." "Stopping growth is not only tyrannical, but against human nature." These common senses rest on myths like "the selfish gene," which purportedly makes each of us crave private control over resources, or the supposedly preordained tragedy of any attempt at commons. Protagonists of other powerful myths include the innately rational *Homo economicus*, always maximizing utility for individual gain, and the fictional self-regulating market. The portrayal of growth-facilitating behaviors as innate, and thus unassailable, works to paralyze the impetus for change. But, surely, we can raise doubts that the natural path to the common good involves selfish greedy individuals competing ruthlessly against one another!

The Case for Degrowth

How has it come to make sense that *everyone* can find satisfaction by "getting ahead"? People mark their success in getting ahead of others by conspicuous consumption of what economists call "positional goods" (depending on context, name-brand clothes, bigger houses, exotic holidays). Economic growth can never provide everyone satisfaction through positional goods, because their value comes from limited accessibility. If everyone owned a Ferrari, the cars would be symbolically equivalent to scooters, giving rise to a demand for more expensive ways to position oneself ahead of others. Most tragically, getting ahead requires leaving (or pushing) others behind, leading to inequalities that undermine the wellbeing of societies, as shown in the extensive evidence cited above.

Moral judgments that validate an individual's struggle to get ahead of others are at odds with those that support mutual aid, reciprocity, and the management of shared resources for common good. Against "greed is natural" and "more is better," degrowth calls for nurturing common senses promoted by enduring cultural and religious traditions around the world, including "share more, lack less" and "enough is enough."

Commons and Commoning

Good living in futures not geared toward growth will require different kinds of relationships among people and with the environments they construct and inhabit. Chapter 3 explores promising approaches through commons – living systems through which groups of people manage and share resources. Commons take the form of forests, fisheries, urban spaces, digital tools, knowledges, technologies, musical repertoires, and more. Commoning is the process through which people collaboratively create, sustain, and enjoy shared resources via communication, regulation, mutual support, conflict negotiation, and experimentation.

Against pushes to privatize and commodify resources – from land and water to healthcare, cultural knowledge, and public spaces – movements to reclaim commons have defended and demanded greater community control. Practicing and modelling shared governance on local scales builds capacity for the larger-scale challenges of managing global commons including air, water, and a habitable earth.

Human survival does not depend only on the material content of commons (fresh water, fish populations, fertile soils, digital tools, health and childcare), but also on the sociocultural systems through which humans (re)produce and manage themselves and their worlds: languages, knowledges, religions, kinship, and other systems. Homo sapiens do not survive alone. Our unique strengths come from our capacities for symbolic thought and communication that allow us to collaboratively generate, sustain, and adapt these common systems.

Degrowth

Ideas and practices of degrowth strive to influence the course of history on two inseparable fronts: halt the growth of material use and market transactions; and build institutions, relationships, and persons to live well without growth. Degrowth calls for slowing down in ways organized to minimize harm to other humans and non-humans. Degrowth seeks to liberate people's time and energy to engage life journeys with patience, compassion, and care for self and others, rather than desperately working more and buying more to escape the pain, sadness, and frustration of finding meaning in the face of life's vulnerabilities. Degrowth is not forced deprivation, but an aspiration to secure enough for everyone to live with dignity and without fear; to experience friendship, love, and health; to be able to give and receive care; and to enjoy leisure and nature.

Degrowth does not claim one unitary theory or plan of action. A remarkably diverse network of thinkers and actors experiment with different initiatives, and engage in healthy debates about what degrowth is, and what forms it can or should take in different contexts. Degrowth analyses reveal detrimental impacts of growth, while degrowth ideals call us to shift productivist ambitions and consumerist identities toward visions of good life characterized by thriving and conviviality among humans and ecosystems.

French thinkers began talking and writing about *décroissance* in the 1970s, and by the dawn of the twenty-first century the idea was sparking political debates and activating a range of local initiatives. Scholarly attention has led to dozens of books and conferences about degrowth, and hundreds of scholarly articles.[15]

Although the term itself first gained traction in Europe, degrowth draws on and engages with enduring and emerging traditions in South America (Buen Vivir), India (Swaraj), and South Africa (Ubuntu), to mention a few.[16] In every corner of the world, individuals and groups have been resisting incursion of growth initiatives into their territories

19

and lives, and struggling to sustain old and to forge new paths away from growth. Ongoing dialogues explore connections and contradictions among these paths.[17]

The interaction of contemporary innovation with ancestral wisdom is evidenced, for example, in Bhutan's commitment to building Gross National Happiness not directed toward GDP growth, but instead toward the attainment of meaning and fulfillment in harmony with Buddhist spiritual values.[18] In parallel processes, millennial Christian traditions of simple communal life are being revitalized in contexts ranging from neo-monastic communities of young evangelicals who eschew consumerism in favor of a collective life of spiritual growth,[19] to Latin America visionaries exploring Pope Francis's call for a radical transition toward integral ecology.[20]

Historical Transformations

Why have scientific facts and arguments demonstrating the negative impacts of growth led to so little change? One limitation is that scientific appeals to individual reason underestimate the power of the sociocultural systems that shape people's ability and willingness to moderate their involvement in expansionist processes. Strategies and motivations for changing course can be strengthened by understanding how current habits of thought and practice emerged and gained dominance.

In his classic history, *The Great Transformation*, Karl Polanyi documents the factors that began to operate in seventeenth-century Britain to reconfigure kinship, religious, moral, and productive systems toward a new world governed by markets and money.[21] Among other outcomes, these processes created a class of workers socialized to sell their labor and to buy provisions. Against millennial traditions in which most humans were socialized to reproduce their families and communities, people had to be goaded to sell their labor. Enclosures of commons that undermined capacities to sustain traditional livelihoods were accompanied by the gendered and racialized manufacture of new kinds of people.

The establishment of racist ideologies and institutions was instrumental to expanding economies in which ethnoracial and colonial hierarchies interact with gender to produce beasts of burden whose labor generates profit for others. For centuries, scientific discourses have been used to identify certain groups of people as inferior, to justify the exploitation of their labor, and to deprive them of their means of (re)production, all supporting the unequal exchanges necessary for the growth of profit. Attempts to challenge inherited gender and racial hierarchies by focusing on individual rights and opportunities are important. But empowering individuals is rarely transformative without attention to the sociocultural systems through which identities, relationships, and worldviews are (re) produced.

Among characteristics unique to the historical complex leading to global growth, individualism is among the most deeply internalized and difficult to address. How to disentangle the roles that individualistic institutions have played in advancing certain rights, freedoms, and equalities from the roles they have played in undermining others, including rights to common management of territories, resources, and cultures for sustaining shared wellbeing?

In US and European populations, one-person households have become the most common type, while the average size of all households has shrunk to between 2 and 2.5 people.[22] The expression of individuality, taste, and success through private homes is a boon for economic growth, fueling the construction of more and more houses and apartments, each with its own furniture, refrigerator, heating system, television, and more. While this trend encourages a gluttonously inefficient use of matter and energy, equally troubling outcomes arise from habitual aloneness. As individuals become detached from the daily joys and struggles of common living, the conviviality of breaking bread, of collaborative care for home and each other, they become more vulnerable to promises of pleasure, meaning, and identity through consumption and competitive display of wealth. This book considers old and new forms of co-living and collaborative provisioning as paths toward reinventing ourselves and our relationships while reclaiming commons.

2

Sacrifices of Growth

The costs of growth at some point become impossibly high. In current conditions, even modest increases in CO_2 emissions will contribute to catastrophic climate shifts.[1] Social limits are also being breached by economies expanding through debt, inequality, and financial crises. Economists and politicians respond to these ills by pushing for more growth. Instead, we identify the problem as growth itself, and argue that the sacrifices made in its pursuit have become intolerable.

The Madness of Compound Growth

Among policy-makers, businesspeople, and lay-persons today, it is common sense that economies should grow at compound rates. A 3 percent

24

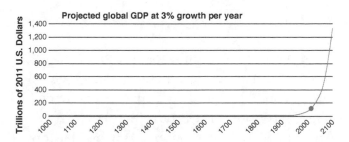

Figure 2.1. Exponential, Compound Growth

Source: G. Kallis, *Degrowth*, London: Agenda Publishing, 2018.
Reproduced with permission.

increase in your salary probably seems reasonable and justified. But sustained GDP growth at that rate is colossal. As noted in Chapter 1, annual 3 percent growth doubles an economy every twenty-four years and, like in the story of the inventor of chess, quickly leads to high magnitudes (Figure 2.1).

Economists learn to call constant GDP growth, even at 3 percent, a "steady-state" rate of growth, even though it causes remarkable acceleration. How can a civilization that takes pride in its rationality rest on the mad idea of an infinitely large economy? To an archeologist in the future, this obsession with growth will seem as strange as Greeks worshipping twelve gods on a mountaintop who masquerade as bulls to have sex, and more deadly than the sacrifice of hundreds of thousands of humans on Aztec pyramids.

You may wonder, don't cities need more bicycles? Don't villages need more potable water? Isn't this growth good? We need to distinguish between the simple expansion of a productive activity and the perpetual growth of economic systems. Historical trajectories of all human populations entail increases and decreases in the production of widely varying goods and services. However, no productive activity can continue to grow endlessly at a compound rate, nor do people want it to. Cities will not benefit from countless bicycles, villagers do not want to be flooded by boundless water, and the perpetual growth of either would exhaust the earth's resources.

In the context of current institutions, what does appear capable of growing without limits is money. David Harvey argues that, without the constraint of gold or other material basis, the world's money supply is simply a set of numbers, spiraling out of control into a bad infinity that can only culminate in devaluation and destruction.[2] For thousands of years, human societies have managed symbolic systems involving money. Although the abstract quality of money makes it susceptible to multiplication, money systems certainly do not require growth to function. Previous civilizations, like Mesopotamia, dynastic China, and classical Greece, kept the scope of money within bounds.[3] In contrast, the socio-economic systems established over the past few centuries motivate and empower the continual reinvestment of money to beget ever more money.

The current historical era, unique in its drive for boundless growth, dawned five centuries ago amid interrelated expansions of European colonization, capital, and racism that established new patterns of human–human and human–environment domination. Shared historical and cultural roots promoting growth continue to influence societies that diverged during the twentieth century along paths labeled capitalism, socialism, and communism. In 1958, the Soviet Union, under Nikita Khrushchev, was actually the first country to announce targets for economic growth (notably 150 percent growth within a decade).[4]

All societies that run after compound growth confront the same unreasonable infinity. In the face of escalating sacrifices and damages, however, different political economic systems offer different possibilities for adaptation. Unlike other human economies, capitalist ones depend on growth. In order to thrive amid market competition, those who have money must invest it, make more money, and expand production. Capitalism without growth is plausible;

in a stagnant, even shrinking, economy, some companies and individuals could continue to profit. But this is hardly a desirable or stable scenario. Once the pie stops growing, anyone who grows their share must do so at the expense of others. Those who get less and less react with increasing desperation, provoking those with greater power to squelch calls for redistribution. Growth's usefulness for maintaining order and stability in capitalist systems motivates conservative and progressive governments alike to pursue growth. Even at considerable costs.

Pursuit of Growth Drives Debt, Inequality, and Financial Crises

Compound growth is unsustainable not only because the planet is finite, but also because growth requires greater sacrifice as each necessary addition gets progressively bigger and bigger. Ever since mid-century growth began to stagnate in the 1970s, governments have tried to minimize production costs by limiting wages, cutting benefits and public services, and weakening unions and labor standards. Meanwhile, they have stimulated consumption with mechanisms like home mortgages and student loans that encourage workers to buy with credit.

Sacrifices of Growth

Starting in the 1980s, the UK, US, and other economies were aggressively re-engineered via neoliberal reforms designed to rekindle growth for the wealthy, with the promise that prosperity would "trickle down" to the rest. Portrayed as liberating markets from burdensome constraints, neoliberal policies are anything but laissez-faire; they redirect regulations, taxes, and public spending on multiple scales.[5] These new rules of the game have helped to sustain growth in the quantities of labor and resources extracted, in market consumption, and in GDPs.

They have also redistributed gains toward the wealthiest, resulting in greater inequalities within and among countries. In the US, average wages have failed to gain purchasing power over forty years, despite a three-fold growth in GDP.[6] Economist Juliet Schor correlates increased consumption during this period with remarkably steep increases in personal debt and average hours worked for pay.[7] These trends have reshaped relationships and subjectivities, contributing to outcomes like higher incidences of depression among people burdened with debt. [8] The bitter irony is that this sacrifice of individual and family wellbeing to boost GDPs in the short term is proving unable to sustain macroeconomic growth over generations.

Growth through debt is a vicious cycle. Economies get indebted to grow, then have to grow to pay back debts. World debt hit a record high of $247,000 trillion in the first quarter of 2018, an 11.1 percent year-on-year increase.[9] Debt repayments by the world's poorest countries have doubled since 2010.[10] International organizations like the IMF and the World Bank guide indebted governments into structural adjustments designed to raise revenues, often by attracting investment from global corporations seeking cheap labor and resources to sustain their own growth.

Global financial crises lay bare the weak foundations of accelerated growth. When the derivatives structures hiding unsound mortgages collapsed in 2007, the US government responded with massive bailouts that saved financial institutions, but failed to prevent widespread pain, dislocation, and conflict around the globe. Whereas analysts and media portray the 2008–10 crisis as resulting from faltering growth, we locate its source in the pursuit of growth in untenable conditions. Countries showing more GDP growth beforehand suffered greater damages and decline during the crisis.[11] Greece and Ireland, for example, whose growth performance surpassing 4 percent was celebrated by the IMF before 2008, collapsed not because they had failed to grow more, but because they had used public and private debt to grow too much.

Short-Sighted Endeavors to Sustain Growth

As economies began to decelerate, with growth rates declining toward zero in cases like Japan and Italy, governments and central banks reacted by pouring money into markets and by cutting public expenditures. The negative impacts of both are unequal and enduring.

Between 2009 and 2019, the European Central Bank pumped almost €2.6 trillion into banks, and the US over €4 trillion – equivalent to its budget for World War II.[12] This "quantitative easing" (in which central banks injected additional money into markets by using newly created reserves to purchase bonds and other assets) was intended together with lowered interest rates to produce additional liquidity, encouraging investment and lending to keep households and economies afloat. Some of the excess money ended up in speculation that perverted commodity, housing, and other markets, leading to devastating outcomes including hunger and homelessness.

Saskia Sassen points to some ominous implications for democracy and civil rights from resulting trends in real estate markets.[13] First was a sharp scale-up in mega-project construction and in corporate and foreign purchase of buildings (in 100 cities worldwide, corporate buying of existing properties exceeded $600 billion from mid-2013 to mid-2014, and $1 trillion a year later). Second were catastrophic levels of foreclosure on modest properties owned by middle-income households (US Federal Reserve data show that over 14 million homeowners lost their homes between 2006 and 2014).

Escalation of housing prices has forced countless residents to leave their homes and cities, to commute long hours to work, or to lose their jobs. Acute crises of homelessness amid meteoric growth are evident in London where, from 2008 to 2014, foreigners bought £100 billion of property,[14] and in San Francisco, where the city with most billionaires per inhabitant is sullied with the feces of residents without homes.[15]

In the face of unplanned stagnation, governments who had counted on growth have imposed austerity measures that reduce spending in realms including health, education, welfare, environment, and salaries. While curbing deficits and freeing up money to pay debts, such cuts undermine the wellbeing and regeneration of a country's most important resource: human beings.

A UN review found that in the UK, the world's fifth largest economy and a center of global finance, austerity cuts had left 14 million people in poverty, and crippled public responses to growing needs around mental health and child poverty.[16] Cuts to European health systems have led to increased infectious diseases and suicides[17] and left rich countries unprepared for dealing with epidemics, despite their formidable resources. Feminists rightly denounce the mounting crises of care, including situations in which all adults in a family must work long hours, while workers paid to care for children, elders, the sick, and homes are underpaid and exploited through gender, ethnoracial, and geographical hierarchies.

In October 2019, Ecuador's president Lenin Moreno decreed a plan for structural adjustment negotiated with the IMF as a precondition for a $4.2 billion loan. Miriam Lang's analysis of the resulting revolt points to recent allotments of around $4 billion in tax cuts and exemptions to large companies with potential to grow Ecuador's GDP.[18] The announced austerity package hit lower-income people by eliminating longstanding fuel subsidies and reducing benefits for public sector workers. When union, indigenous, student, and other groups erupted in protest, the government declared a state of emergency, sending thousands of military personnel and heavy equipment onto the streets. Twelve days of conflict resulted in eight deaths, an estimated 1,300 injuries and 1,200 detentions, and the withdrawal of the austerity package.

In sum, onerous debt, forced austerity, and wild inflation in food and housing markets are all portrayed as maladies to be cured by growth. We argue, to the contrary, that these are all consequences of policies intended to stimulate growth.

Ecological Costs of Growth

Growing economies require constant inputs of resources, and constantly transform land, water, and air shared with other species. Environmental scientists designate our era as "the great acceleration." Plot any graph of historical change in global environmental impacts (carbon dioxide emissions, water use, ocean acidification, waste dumping, etc.) and you will find a hockey stick figure in which an almost horizontal line shows little change over centuries, and then, as in Figure 2.1, impacts accelerate during the twentieth century to a nearly vertical line. The similarity with the hockey stick of GDP is not a coincidence; acceleration of GDP is what accelerates environmental impacts.

Coal miners used to take canaries into the mines. When too much carbon monoxide accumulated, the canary would expire, warning the miners to retreat. What will it take for us to pay attention to contemporary canaries? Bird populations across the French countryside have fallen by a third over the past fifteen years, due to pesticides and other factors.[19] In the US, 3.5 million bee colonies have been lost from the 6 million counted in 1947.[20] For the 2019 UN report on biodiversity and ecosystem services, 145 scientists from fifty countries reviewed 15,000 scientific studies, concluding that "nature is declining globally at rates unprecedented in human history – and the rate of species extinctions is accelerating, with grave impacts on people around the world now likely."[21] Reduction of biodiversity worldwide, interacting with industrial-scale farming and habitat loss, threatens to increase the frequency of disease outbreaks such as COVID-19.[22]

Growing economies also mean growing waste and emissions. At current rates, by 2050 the oceans will contain more plastic than fish.[23] Despite knowledge of the consequences of climate breakdown, global emissions growth increased from 1 percent a year in the 1990s to 3 percent per year in this millennium. Nations that committed in the 2015 Paris Agreement to keep global temperature change within 1.5° C are now on track for a devastating 4° C warming.[24]

The correlation between GDP and carbon emissions is not incidental. Current scales of economic production are made possible by fossil fuels. A 1 percent difference in GDP among countries is associated with a 0.6–1 percent difference in CO_2 emissions.[25] To limit temperature increases to 1.5° C, the IPCC says global carbon emissions must be nearly halved by 2030. All viable scenarios involve dramatic decrease in global energy use.

Responsibilities and responses are complicated by extreme differences among countries in terms of benefits and burdens of growth, and by the substantial ecological debt owed by societies who have, in recent centuries, consumed disproportionate amounts of global resources and produced more than their fair share of emissions and waste.

Exploitation: Vital Ingredient for Growth

The social and ecological costs of growth are systemic, not incidental. Growth results from surplus invested to make more surplus. Surplus is obtained by selling a product or service for more than the costs of labor and resources used to produce it. So, arranging cheap access to workers, materials, and energy is essential for growth. Production chains and accounting systems that shift costs and damages onto distant environments, other people, and future generations are pervasive features of growth economies.

Technological change is instrumental, but not sufficient, for economic growth. Eighteenth-century British inventors repeatedly adapted spinning wheels and looms to enable the production of more cloth in less time. However, these innovations only activated growth in combination with the underpaid labor of factory workers, the unpaid labor of enslaved Africans growing cotton in the Americas, the women who reproduced and cared for both groups, and cheap access to land (soil, water, lumber, etc.) expropriated from natives in the same territories. Even these conditions could not lead to market growth without expanding demand. Sven Beckert documents aggressive British moves to create new markets for cloth, notably by undermining artisanal networks producing silk and other garments in India.[26]

Beckert also shows that, before the twentieth century, only a tiny portion of people worldwide exchanged labor for wages. Most toiled for family subsistence, some as feudal dependents, others as enslaved laborers. The difficulty in persuading people to sell their labor is evidenced by forms of coercion exercised on various scales and regions. In Europe and its colonies, traditional livelihoods were undermined through widely ranging mechanisms employed to expropriate local commons, while new kinds of people were manufactured through changing social institutions. Two enduring mechanisms evolved to engineer (and to justify) forms of exploitation vital to economic expansion: appropriation through racialization, and gendered hierarchization of production versus reproduction.

Arrangements established during the industrial revolution to exploit men's, women's, and children's labor ran into crises of sustainability. From English textile mills to American plantations there were challenges in sustaining human resources amid high rates of illness, disability, disappearance, and death. Wage-workers and enslaved people alike were unable or unwilling to fulfill the demands of productive labor and simultaneously bear, raise, and care for new generations of workers.

Over several centuries, a historic mode of gendered (re)production evolved to cheaply supply, sustain, *and* reproduce labor for expanding economies. Silvia Federici uncovers violent historical processes that established women as machines to (re)produce human resources,[27] while equally violent processes established certain groups of men as machines to produce profit for others.[28] In changes that achieved phenomenal reach, the new mode of wage labor came to be associated with masculinity, labeled "productive," and rewarded with money, prestige, and other resources denied to "reproductive" labor, increasingly associated with femininity.

Growth via exploitation is rife with contradictions. Paying workers less lowers production costs; it also limits their ability to stay healthy and to buy products. Socializing women to reproduce workers and to provide unpaid daily care effectively subsidizes the cost of hired labor; it also complicates efforts to incorporate those women into the labor market. Cheaper techniques for exploiting resources reduce production costs; they often increase degradation and pollution. Maximizing masculine-identified productive labor enhances growth; it also undermines the feminine-associated care work and knowledge necessary to sustain families, communities, and environments.

Amid these tensions and contradictions, interacting with organized struggles to improve labor conditions, forms of human and animal power were progressively substituted with a bonanza of cheap power from fossil fuels. In the nineteenth and twentieth centuries, first coal, then oil, together with petrochemical inputs, significantly increased manufacturing output per labor hour and agricultural yields per unit of land. Fossil-fueled transportation subsidized increasingly multi-sited arrangements for production and consumption, the relocation of sites for underpaid and enslaved laborers, and the expansion of consumer markets worldwide. These developments were instrumental in shifting economies toward compound growth.

Pursuit of fossil fuels and new markets has activated geopolitical power to facilitate exploitation of weaker countries. Mechanisms ranging from development programs to outright war helped to forge global markets and supply chains at enormous cost to diverse traditions and value systems. After Harry Truman's 1949 inaugural address foregrounded international development in US foreign policy, the World Bank labeled two thirds of the world's people as "poor" and in need of development. Invaluable ways of being and relating were steamrollered by the expansion of Euro-American institutions and lifeways. As a 1951 UN report lamented, "rapid economic progress is impossible without painful adjustments. Ancient philosophies have to be scrapped; old social institutions have to disintegrate; bonds of caste, creed and race have to burst; and large numbers of persons who cannot keep up with progress have to have their expectations of a comfortable life frustrated. Very few communities are willing to pay the full price of economic progress."[29]

In sum, growth has been enabled by hierarchical sociocultural systems that support unequal exchanges of labor and other resources between people, between countries, and between humans and their natural environments. Gendered expectations have interacted with evolving racial, class, and colonial hierarchies to minimize the costs of producing, sustaining, and exploiting humans. The sacrifice of diverse preexisting identities and relations leaves deeply felt legacies.

Psycho-Social Foundations of Growth

Growth is not an external force that befalls innocent humans; socioeconomic systems are (re)produced every day by people's actions and attitudes. The necessity to sell one's labor to survive shapes people's perceptions and desires. When you compete with others for limited opportunities to earn a living, you welcome market expansion. When recessions bring unemployment and debts, you support any move to prop up growth.

In individualistic societies and anonymous urban environments, people learn to signal their worth and status by what they buy in comparison to others. This is not just a question of vanity. It is a matter of self-esteem and dignity in environments where respect requires obtaining what those around you consider decent clothes, homes, vehicles, or medical treatment.

Experiences of insecurity and inadequacy have been harnessed to drive growing consumption, with heavy psychological costs. As rich and poor run faster and faster to meet expectations and compete with one another, the economy accelerates, in turn exacerbating time-anxiety and exhaustion. Promises that economic growth will bring a life of convenience, with little pain or obligation, appeal to many, including ourselves. The obvious problem is that growth that depends on inequality and exploitation can only bring this dream to a privileged few. Deeper problems, explored in the following chapter, stem from the shallowness of moral and human meaning in a life spent chasing individual privilege, free of limits and community commitments.

To keep systemic expansion going, growth imperatives are internalized in life purposes and identities, making it feel like the impetus for growth is in our DNA. But individual competitiveness, selfish hoarding, the desire to control property, and the insatiable urge to consume are not hardwired survival instincts. These behaviors have been fostered in recent history to serve the expansion of specific economic systems. Human nature offers many possibilities: we can be selfish and we can be altruistic, we can want more and we can do well with less, we can accumulate but also share. Which propensities get cultivated and which ones constrained depends on sociocultural systems.

The evolutionary feature that has assured survival throughout the lifetime of our species is a biophysical capacity for symbolic thought and communication that enables groups of humans to collaboratively develop languages, religions, kinship, and other eco-social systems that survive the individual organism, and that help to produce new generations of humans, their habits, and their habitats. These common systems enable humans to shape all kinds of worlds. We now explore some types of human organization that can foster a transition to degrowth, together with spirits and subjectivities that form and are nourished by them.

3

Making Changes
on the Ground

Narratives that dominate contemporary life make it easier to imagine the end of the world, even the end of capitalism, than the end of growth. How do we begin to think of other ways forward? By observing and appreciating what already exists. People in every part of the world inherit, adapt, and invent alternatives to predominant economic models and mindsets. Many draw on long-evolving traditions that celebrate living simply in solidarity with others.

Here we build a case for degrowth from the ground up, learning from people who embody and perform everyday common senses in the spirit of degrowth. This differs from global programs to curb biodiversity loss and climate change, but we do not see them as mutually exclusive. Without the daily exercise of sharing food, homes, neighborhoods, and thoughtful conversation, we humans cannot develop the capacities to make and carry out international climate treaties and Green New Deals.

This chapter begins by looking at lives guided by values of community wellbeing, rather than competition and growth. It then considers cases in which people have come together in collaborative ventures, and asks how these processes lead to broader transitions. Key here are concepts introduced in Chapter 1: commons, defined as living systems of shared resources; and commoning, conceived as exercises of collaboration, conflict, and deliberation that sustain and adapt traditions and regulations.

Commoning can be oriented toward growth or degrowth, toward defending the status quo or enacting change through performative rearticulations of common sense. Highlighting the potential to push against forces of privatization, David Bollier advocates strengthening and extending common systems of provisioning and care as alternatives to debt-driven economies catering to unquenchable demands for growth.[1] We urge greater appreciation of forms of care and social reproduction that have long sustained and coexisted with wage labor and market goods. And we seek to learn from common modes of production and consumption including communal food gardens, community supported agriculture, and agroecology networks;

ecocommunes, co-living and co-housing arrangements; peer-to-peer software, hardware, and digital commons; and co-parenting and childcare circles.

These commons, and the lives of the commoners who make them, are rife with contradictions. In institutional and ideological environments adapted to support and defend private property and competition, efforts to forge and sustain collaborative ventures inevitably require struggles and raise doubts. This is why mutual nourishment is so vital among networks of collaborators, together with the adaptation of policies, institutions, and resource structures to create more propitious conditions.

The Common Sense of Sharing and Living Simply So That Others May Simply Live

Across the world, popular culture, media, and education promote hard work, hard play, competition, and individual achievement displayed through production and consumption. Coexisting with these powerful messages are other logics and desires rooted in traditions that foster simpler, gentler paths lived in solidarity with those who have different needs. Meaning and pleasure are variously enjoyed through song, dance, sport, or prayer;

sharing meals or conversation; watching sunsets or strolling the landscape. These common senses inspire and sustain diverse paths toward degrowth.

The few world leaders who embody such senses stand out. Think of Pope Francis, who eschewed the palatial papal residence in favor of a hostel suite, and who walked the midnight streets of Rome in disguise in order to talk, sit, and eat with men and women without homes. Or the former president of Uruguay, José Mujica, who passed up the presidential palace to live at his humble farm on the outskirts of Montevideo, while donating 90 percent of his presidential salary. Such behavior is marked as abnormal in societies where dominant expectations of masculinity are achieved through displays of wealth, power, and status. In contrast, countless women's lives exemplifying degrowth sensibilities go unremarked in contexts where good womanhood is defined by modesty and abnegation of personal ambition in favor of commitment to family and community. One woman who has gained visibility is Winona LaDuke, the Harvard-trained economist who twice ran for US vice-president with the Green Party. Through most of her adult life, LaDuke has lived modestly on the Ojibwe White Earth Reservation in Minnesota, joining daily practices of farming and gathering among extended family as a basis for leadership in environmental struggles.

Innumerable others practice modest living: city folks who find contentment in work, family, or friends without striving for ever-greater wealth and power; farmers who produce enough to reproduce their communities without exhausting natural resources; pensioners dedicated to community work; artisans and petty producers by choice. Alongside those who choose to live simply in complex societies are millions who live simply out of tradition or necessity. In a special issue of the *Journal of Political Ecology*, Gezon and Paulson bring together researchers from numerous cultural and linguistic backgrounds who write about these varied processes in thirteen countries.[2]

People living low-impact lives not driven toward growth make up a good share of the world population. Unfortunately, gentle and sustainable local living does not always guarantee peace. On the frontiers of expanding extractive economies, people living with very low levels of consumption are risking their lives to resist economic developments.[3] Notable examples come from the Zapatistas who, since rising up in 1994 (on the day the North American Free Trade Agreement went into effect), have blocked growth-driven initiatives advanced by the Mexican government, including a mega-highway project designed to expand agribusiness and ecotourism in Chiapas.[4] Rather than claiming a larger piece of Mexico's economic pie, Zapatistas (like other groups, including the Kurds) fight for the right to forge their own paths.

Some members of global elites have traveled to Chiapas to show solidarity and to learn from traditional lifeways. Others respond to yearnings for simplicity with meditation, Tai chi, yoga, minimalist design, decluttering, tiny houses, and early retirement. Positions of privilege through which these longings are experienced should not blind us to the desires they express for moving toward less harmful and more meaningful lives.

People trying to make positive changes are often condemned as hypocritical: "She rides her bike to work to reduce emissions, then jets off to climate summits." "They help the poor, financed by corporate dividends." Harsh critiques from the pro-growth mainstream, and also from purist activists, function as reactionary defenses against any variation from the status quo. Demands that a person's every action be fully consistent with a defined value-set effectively paralyze impulses for innovation. Short of abandoning everything to live in a cave, none of us can try out options without contradicting existing lifestyles designed to facilitate growth. As the saying goes, if you have more than seven contradictions you are a hypocrite, if you have less than four, a fanatic.

From Personal to Common

It is naive to think about change, however, as a question of individual volition. Our abilities to change are circumscribed by material conditions and internalized worldviews and ideologies. Efforts to unlearn embodied habits and mindsets – ranging from admiration for idols, billionaires, and bling, to the mundane routines of buying a burger or using a car – raise tensions and meet resistance.

What conditions enable or constrain our capacities to question personal sacrifices of growth, experienced as stress, competition, overwork, and loneliness, or as obsessions with income, wealth, publications, cars, clothes, food, drugs, and alcohol? What supports us to embrace and construct other lifeways? Reflecting on processes that we have lived and studied in rural and urban places ranging from Bolivia and India to Greece and Spain, we highlight one aspect of the answer: being and becoming in common.

Individuals trying to forge various paths toward shared wellbeing often connect with each other in practice and conversation, forming networks where common senses of moderation, self-limitation, and solidarity are performed, and where political commitments take form. Mutual encouragement to try small changes, together with organized support to sustain and benefit from such changes, can counterbalance those paralyzing accusations of hypocrisy. With time, some collaborative practices engender shared visions that fuel collective action to change institutions and environments.

Faced with the vast environmental damage provoked by growing economies, the minuscule amount of mitigation achieved by one person eating less meat, commuting by bike, or sharing more can be discouraging. Yet supporting each other to bring about desired worlds is vitally important because it changes us, nurturing ways of being and becoming that have broad social and political repercussions. Taking personal action is a first step toward building societies that implement needed changes in policies and institutions.

Coevolutionary Possibilities

If you live in a North American suburb and work miles from home, car-driving seems the only reasonable option. If you live in Copenhagen, sur-rounded by beautiful bike-paths, it is easier to cycle to work or school, together with 49 percent of the population.[5] Such conducive environments coevolve in dynamics among personal desires and habits, net-works, and changing institutions. A start is people who want to bike for health, budget, environmen-tal, or other reasons. These people may connect with each other and organize initiatives ranging from group pleasure-rides to DIY workshops, voting for pro-biking candidates, and protests to reclaim public space. As authorities respond (for example, with policies and programs to add bike lanes, bike-sharing, or reduce car traffic or speed in certain areas), more people can commute safely by bike, develop the strengths and skills to enjoy biking, and come to prefer cycling over driving. In cities like Malmö, Montreal, and Tokyo, this virtu-ous cycle has made the growth of bike-commuting a civic and political priority.

Organic processes like these inevitably reflect the social orders from which they arise. Attention to ways in which some cycling advocacy movements have excluded non-white and low-income people and interests, or exacerbated gentrification, helps provoke conscious efforts to recognize and reach across different positions and powers.

Making Changes on the Ground

Crises can catalyze personal changes, open cracks in dominant norms and expectations, and bring people together to reinvent themselves and their relationships. Angelos Varvarousis explains how, between 2009 and 2016, many Greeks disoriented by prolonged crisis found meaning in cooperative projects ranging from urban gardens, time-banks, and collective art centers to solidarity clinics and food banks.[6] The collapse of mass consumption and the crisis of the welfare state destabilized identities that have long been experienced as natural. Ephemeral common experiences, such as mass occupation of public plazas or impromptu planting of gardens, acted as rites of passage for participants transitioning from a past no longer viable to a future yet to be defined. In the practical work of producing new commons, people experiment with new selves and relations.

Likewise, *Guardian* journalist George Monbiot notes how, amid the coronavirus crisis, and despite measures of physical distancing, commons of mutual aid and care have exploded all over the world in projects that support the poor and vulnerable, care for doctors and care workers, or provide low-cost technological solutions to hospitals in need of specialized equipment.[7]

In Puerto Rico, as a result of self-governing

processes developed over thirty-five years around an anti-mining movement, everyday performances in common projects have nurtured common senses around nature, community, and democracy that have changed participants in ways that counter prevalent common senses of growth.[8] In sum, coevolution can happen when individuals innovate and connect with others, and together perform new kinds of relationships that prefigure political change on other scales. Thus, emerging networks become forces for institutional change, both modelling and advocating different structures of governance.

Commons That are Already Here

The money economy is the tip of an iceberg sustained by immense activity organized in voluntary, reciprocal, and not-for-profit forms.[9] Time-use studies in Australia and elsewhere reveal that as many hours are devoted to household and care work (performed largely by women) as to paid employment.[10] In 2010 in Catalonia, sociologists Joana Conill, Manuel Castells, and their colleagues found that the significant portions of time people dedicated to activities not involving monetary exchange included mutual favors, fixing their own or their friends' houses or cars, growing or preparing food, or engaging in voluntary organizations.[11] What happens if governments counterbalance the enormous investments made to bolster money economies with an increasing appreciation of and support for the skills, values, and strategies exercised in the arrangement of childcare, the sharing of home-grown produce or baked goods, continual attention to ill and elderly members, and the clean up of neighborhood streets and parks?

These unheralded commons provide foundations for reconstructing economies oriented toward goals other than growth. The globalization of one monoculture based on selfish competition seems to have undermined myriad forms of mutual aid that have propelled social evolution throughout history. Yet, a plurality of embodied common senses, some contradicting others, always allow human individuals and communities to adapt their values and views of the world around them.

The good news is that enduring ethics and systems of community and environmental care that have been undervalued and exploited by market growth are giving rise to new forms of collaboration. Not isolated sanctuaries or exit utopias, these arrangements intertwine with existing economies in various ways.

Community Economies in Coevolution

The city of Barcelona, where three of us live, abounds with commoning arrangements. The Catalan Integral Cooperative (CIC), for example, interconnects diverse productive ventures and hundreds of self-employed people, with an annual budget of around $480,000.[12] Through its Catalan Supply Centre, small producers deliver some 4,500 pounds of food each month to twenty-one spaces self-managed by consumers. CIC issues its own currency, Faircoin, provided as a basic income to members, and funds new cooperative ventures through its self-financing interest-free bank with 155 members and $250,000 in deposits. CIC's most audacious project is the post-industrial colony of Calafou: a 28,000 msq abandoned factory 60 km outside Barcelona, that twenty-two members rented and developed into twenty-seven units including a hacklab and a soap production lab, carpentry and mechanical workshops, and a professional music studio.

Interconnecting some 110,000 people, supporting 6,000 to earn money and 300 enterprises in the Solidarity Economy Network,[13] Barcelona's cooperative ecosystem allows residents with different political and personal sensibilities to dedicate some of their energies to constructing worlds they desire. You can become a member of Som Energia, which will deliver 100 percent renewable electricity to your home at affordable cost; share an electric car through Som Mobilitat; connect to the internet through Som Connexio; receive primary care through the COS health cooperative; live in a co-housing unit built by the architect cooperative Sostre Civic; take turns in a parent-run childcare group; grow vegetables in a community garden; buy produce from a local farmer through membership in a consumer cooperative; or listen to new bands in citizen-run social centers called Ateneus.

Barcelona's history of cooperativism is unique, yet resonates with community economies worldwide. In Mississippi, Cooperation Jackson has developed similarly to CIC. In the Phoenix Commons self-managed co-housing community for over-55s in Oakland, California, residents share communal areas, including a kitchen where rotating committees prepare shared meals.[14] Worldwide, hundreds of eco-communes, transition towns, co-living and co-housing communities are learning together and gaining strength in national and global associations.

People practicing less damaging and wasteful ways of producing and accessing food are also banding together at various scales. The international peasants' network Via Campesina represents 182 small farmer organizations in eighty-one countries around a mission to facilitate collaborative learning, exchange, and organizing among individuals and groups exercising and experimenting with healthy and sustainable forms of agriculture.

Limits and Doubts

Are we proposing to feed nine billion people with urban gardens, lodge everyone in co-housing, and raise the world's children in neighborhood circles? Indeed not: we encourage support for cooperative modes of production, consumption, and caring in order to complement and renew large-scale public arrangements and forms of private use or ownership.

The goal is not to replace one monoculture with another. It is to create conditions that support the development of more vibrant realms of possibility with different rhythms, purposes, and scales. Today's political systems promote and subsidize a growth-driven model based on private property, paid labor, and market consumption, leaving other arrangements underappreciated, undernourished, and overexploited. Our strategy is to re-order values and resources to support the development of diverse life-making processes operating with different logics. That diversity will be key to resilience and adaptation in the face of historical-environmental challenges.

Does the case for degrowth reject technological advancements, marking a retrogression to the grueling labor of earlier times? On the contrary, we recognize the role that large-scale high-tech production will continue to play, and observe that many smaller processes, including those oriented toward purposes other than growth, are also strengthened by technological innovations.

Across Latin America, small farmers in agroecology organizations combine traditional practices with cutting-edge scientific knowledge.[15] Time-bankers in New Zealand use computer programs to record and calculate in-kind contributions.[16] Vassilis Kostakis points to initiatives at the interface of digital and physical production, and of local manufacture and global design and distribution: L'Atelier Paysan (France) and Farmhack (US and UK) build open-source agricultural machines for small-scale farming; Wikihouse democratizes the construction of sustainable, resource-light dwellings; OpenBionics produces open-source designs for robotic and bionic devices; and the RepRap community creates replicable designs for 3D printers.[17]

These examples integrate recent innovations in science and engineering with longstanding modes of human organization in small-scale, decentralized, and locally controlled production arrangements that strive to minimize hierarchy and exploitation.

Will collective forms of provisioning and care be exploited to subsidize growth economies? Yes, sharing activities that generate value can be captured and coopted by the market, as new commons open up opportunities for new enclosures. In the meteoric rise of networks for sharing rides, homes, tools, skills, food, and favors, for example, models supporting equitable sharing coexist with for-profit exploitation. Both can contribute to reducing material use, while enacting quite different power relations. There is also the danger that corporations and states will seek to buffer losses by shifting even more welfare costs on to uncommodified family and social life. In some contexts, the model of women performing unpaid reproductive labor to subsidize men's wage work is already being replaced by one in which the underpaid work of women and men is subsidized by collaborative efforts to supply nourishment, healthcare, childcare, and elder-care.

Temptations to romanticize communities and idealize social movements should not blind us to instances in which community-driven action is exclusionary toward outsiders and tyrannical toward its members. Communal projects must negotiate inclusion and exclusion, horizontal and vertical relations, as they address tensions and contradictions in the consolidation of common values and meanings. The model unfolded here across several chapters bolsters this journey by articulating ongoing community-building with changes in state institutions and in personal practices and values.

In today's world, pre-growth and post-growth forms of organization inevitably coexist with enterprises and social systems developed to support growth, promising conflict and contradiction, as well as complementarity. Power dynamics engineered in the growth era, including racism, sexism, and classism, will continue to shadow journeys toward more equitable lifeways. It takes time, collaborative reflection, and courage to adapt deeply internalized identities and relations. Efforts to value the means as much as the ends can generate processes that are rewarding in themselves. Even initiatives that fail to fulfill their original goals have afterlives in the form of persons, relationships, and networks enriched and evolved along the way.

Day by Day Transformation to Degrowth

In the examples presented above, people come together to provide for practical and spiritual needs in ways that prioritize community and environmental wellbeing. They are adapting long-evolving traditions together with new technologies and ventures in ways that nourish experiences and cultivate communities. How do these day by day exercises of provisioning and governance change politics and societies?

Although most of the initiatives described here are not pursued in the name of degrowth, we understand them as prefiguring degrowth transitions. First, permeated by a spirit of living simply within one's means and in community, they nourish and elevate the common senses with which we started this chapter. Second, activity is directed to the needs and wellbeing of workers and users, not the generation of profit. Third, these initiatives promote models of community ownership and production based on sharing and cooperation. Fourth, many produce less negative socioecological impacts than existing market systems thanks to slower paces, lower material and energy use, and more re-circulation within local economies. While they may look less productive in profit terms, these initiatives are productive in creating jobs and enhancing human-environmental wellbeing.

Cooperative experiments anticipate desired worlds by exercising and consolidating real options that societies may build on as socioecological crises escalate and money economies falter. In the following chapter, we outline a set of policies that can establish fertile conditions for strengthening diverse modes of provisioning and for cultivating common senses and identities. The institutional and structural changes proposed there are motivated by people described here, already thinking and living in different ways.

Bodily practices and shared experiences socialize participants and generations in varying ways of being and interrelating. By cultivating plots in urban gardens, people come to better appreciate the challenges and seasonality of food production. They may feel more solidarity with farmers, be less likely to waste food, and more eager to eat whole foods in season. Participants in cooperative projects may move beyond the role of client of commercial providers; rather than addressing grievances to distant power-holders, they become participants in building conditions in which they want to live.

Through regular corporal practices, we humans build muscle memory. Our patterns of language, practice, and thought shape the ways our brains develop. So, by exercising our bodies and minds in specific ways, and by engaging and teaching others to do so, we continually produce ourselves and new generations. Large and small adjustments to habits of thought, action, and interaction work in mysterious ways toward institutional and paradigmatic change.

As collective bodies and minds change, the personal becomes political. An individual's voluntary shift from a weekend spent shopping abroad to one picking olives with friends in a community grove, from an evening watching TV to one playing with neighborhood children, may not directly slow the global growth machine, nor revert climate change. However, new habits alter the ways we develop human potential day by day, thereby influencing environments through which family, neighbors, students, colleagues, and others continually develop their potentials. Producing new kinds of people and relationships is fundamental to any cultural transformation and great transition.

4

Path-Breaking Reforms

Policy and institutional changes are outcomes and drivers of coevolution. Societies where common senses already encourage low-impact lives oriented toward wellbeing support reforms to advance degrowth. In turn, timely and crucial policy interventions create spaces for degrowth-oriented common senses and commons infrastructures to develop.

In this chapter we propose five types of reforms that can work together to favor futures where common people work, produce, and consume less, share more, enjoy more free time, and live with dignity and joy. These policy packages are: a Green New Deal without growth; universal incomes and services; policies to reclaim the commons; reduction of working hours; and public finance that supports the first four. Recognizing that these proposals will be designed and applied differently in different cultural, geographic, and political contexts and at various scales, they are outlined here in ways relevant for OECD countries.

We start from proposals that people are already contemplating or trying out, and that are slowly becoming common sense. After our grand critique of growth systems, it might seem anticlimactic to look at programs currently advanced by political parties in various countries. First, however, it is a plus, not a minus, to draw from and build on agendas in which serious thought, debate, and experimentation have been invested. Second, while these proposals may be moderate when employed to advance the goals of stabilizing or greening growth societies, they become radical when oriented toward managing without growth. Integrated into missions to maintain wellbeing while reducing resource use and environmental damage, these reforms would change the very structure of the system.

A Green New Deal Without Growth

Green New Deals (GNDs) proposed in the US, EU, and globally, integrate social and economic reforms and public works projects to address socioeconomic and environmental challenges simultaneously. Our degrowth vision coincides with the integrated approach of GNDs, and with most of the objectives specified in the 2019 US congressional resolution summarized here: (A) achieve net-zero greenhouse gas emissions through a fair and just transition; (B) create millions of good, high-wage jobs and ensure prosperity and economic security for all people; (C) invest in infrastructure and industry to sustainably meet the challenges of the twenty-first century; (D) secure for all people for generations to come: clean air and water; climate and community resiliency; healthy food; access to nature; and a sustainable environment; (E) promote justice and equity by stopping current, preventing future, and repairing historic oppression of frontline and vulnerable communities.[1]

Yet, there are some important differences between proposals for GNDs and for degrowth. In current conversations, GND proposals link fulfillment of their objectives to green growth and prosperity, widely understood as increased income and material wealth. In contrast, degrowth recognizes that more income for all means rising GDPs, which correlate with increased environmental damage. The GND proposal for Europe draws attention to this dilemma by also calling for "ending the dogma of endless growth," abandoning GDP growth as the primary measure of progress, and focusing instead on what matters: "health, happiness and the environment."[2]

Degrowth and GNDs share commitments to the rapid and massive deployment of renewable energy; the decarbonization of transport and agriculture; the refurbishment and provision of new zero-carbon affordable housing; reforestation and ecological restoration. But degrowth goes further to recognize that, in growth economies, even an expansion of renewable energy brings growing costs and risks. To foster a just distribution of costs and benefits, including to communities where energy sources are located or materials extracted, the plan for the European GND includes an Environmental Justice Commission. Supporting this move, degrowth also promotes the most fundamental way to reduce socioecological costs: use less total energy.

Powerful political resistance has been rallied around fears that energy transition will slash jobs and income from sectors dependent on fossil fuels. Partly in response to those pressures, proponents emphasize the potential of GNDs to function as economy-wide stimuli, creating new jobs and new consumption in green sectors. Making sure workers can transition from dirty to clean industries is also crucial in degrowth visions. Rather than high incomes for all, however, our fourth policy package supports high employment without growth through decent wages for all, with less hours worked by each.

How can ambitious GND proposals be funded without growth? Our fifth policy package outlines public finance options to raise or reallocate resources for all four proposals. To launch GNDs, governments could issue GND-specific bonds, possibly through public green banks, paid back with returns from the projects themselves in arrangements that do not require the economy as a whole to grow.[3] Pension funds could invest in GND projects, keeping money in the public realm, and central banks could buy part of the bonds, in effect a reverse quantitative easing.

Universal Basics

Universal Basic Services (UBS) and Universal Basic Income (UBI) aim to establish conditions for all members of society to live with dignity and health. In doing so, they also aim to recognize unpaid contributions to society and to generate grounds for various forms of collaboration.

UBS provide education and healthcare for all, together with affordable access to food, housing, and public transportation. Economists at London University's Global Prosperity Institute have developed a plan for guaranteed housing, food, transport, and internet access that would cost the equivalent of 2.3 percent of the UK's GDP, an amount that could be raised by eliminating two thirds of the tax breaks currently available.[4]

UBI is an income paid to each resident in a municipality, state, or country. By definition universal and unconditional, UBI replaces the stigma and bureaucratic inefficiencies associated with current proof-based assistance such as unemployment relief. In OECD economies, a basic income for adults, set at 15–22.5 percent of the average per capita income, could be funded with a moderate increase in taxes for the richest 10–15 percent, and a deduction of the benefits replaced by basic income.[5]

Louise Haagh observes that a basic income has been advocated from remarkably wide-ranging ideological positions and combined with dissimilar political actions.[6] Karl Widerquist, who has long promoted UBI to enhance "the freedom to say no" to exploitative wage relations, assesses varying designs and approaches to basic income, together with lessons learned from experiments underway in Canada, Finland, Kenya, the US and UK.[7]

How and for what purposes UBIs are implemented matters. Some applications aim to subsidize growth by mitigating poverty and improving productivity. Degrowth aligns with other proposals seeking material conditions that can liberate individuals from exploitative employment, support transformation away from environmentally damaging regimes,[8] and help move beyond battles of jobs vs. environment toward politics that address viable livelihoods as inseparable from a sustainable earth.[9]

In dialogue with radical feminists, we propose a Universal Care Income that builds on other expressions of UBI, but differs by foregrounding the social recognition of unpaid and highly gendered care work that we all perform to sustain the life and wellbeing of households and communities.[10] Care Income seeks to foster equity and solidarity by conceptualizing the universal income as an investment out of common wealth in the contributions and capacities of all of us to take care of ourselves, our kin, and others.

At the heart of degrowth is a collective endeavor to make life viable and enjoyable through material and meaningful support not driven toward profit. Universal basics support degrowth transformations by distributing the wealth of nations through means other than market mechanisms, and by maintaining modest material security for everyone during transitions to slower and less marketized economies. These policies promote shared services, such as public transportation, that are vital for reducing resource use and carbon emissions, and help to transcend perceived conflicts between jobs and environments. Finally, universal basics enhance people's freedom to explore different lifestyles and to choose how to devote their time and their care.

Reclaiming the Commons

Local and national policies have worked wonders to commodify and privatize almost everything, and they can work equally well to promote cooperative production, provisioning, and living.

Services such as water, energy, waste management, transportation, education, health, or childcare could be run as municipal or consumer cooperatives rather than for-profit businesses. The 2019 bankruptcy of Pacific Gas and Electric Company in the wake of California fires sparked mobilization around proposals for a customer-owned utility that would put users on the board overseeing the company's management, and dramatically reduce costs by eliminating the need to pay dividends to shareholders. Relieved of their profit-making purpose, systems like utilities and housing can be gradually re-conceptualized as common goods, produced and regenerated through collaborative governance.

Barcelona is one among many cities actively working to promote commons. TheBarcelona En Comú (Barcelona in Common – BiC) citizen's platform that has governed the city since 2015 expanded the focus of a municipal innovation agency, Barcelona Activa (initially an incubator for private businesses), to include enhancement of human resources and networks supporting the solidarity economy and commons-based businesses. In government, BiC adapted public procurement standards to prioritize sustainability and social responsibility; legislated that 30 percent of all new housing should be social, making available 1,222 new, low-cost apartments; promoted co-ownership schemes for new social houses built on municipal land; extended the biking network to 250 kms; and ceded unused public spaces to neighborhood cooperatives. A municipal electricity distributor, Barcelona Energía, was set up to use solar power produced on municipal premises to supply public buildings.

Spaces can be reclaimed for the public and, where

relevant, turned into commons through a range of interventions, including lifting earlier interventions designed to privatize and profit from public realms. Examples include converting unused lots into squares or parks, removing fees and barriers to accessing natural areas (coasts, forests, mountains), recovering underused public or abandoned private buildings for use by neighborhood associations or cooperatives. Low-cost innovations can lead to remarkable improvements in wellbeing. Consider the superblocks program in Barcelona, a grid of basic roads forming 400 by 400 meter polygons, closed to motorized vehicles and street parking. A superblock costs little more than a few traffic signs, improves the quality of life and health of residents, and stimulates neighborhood economies.[11]

In varying contexts and at different scales, legislation, subsidies, and tax breaks currently designed to boost private profits can be realigned to support social and solidarity enterprises and cooperatives. Options include jurisdictional formalization; training and assistance for commons-based start-ups; prioritization in public procurement; funds set up with ethical banks; tax or social security breaks; transitioning bankrupt companies to workers' ownership, and more.[12]

Some of our most important commons are the

sanitation, health, and care commons that provide resilience against disease and epidemics. On these fronts, degrowth prioritizes networks of care, solidarity, and support, both local and translocal; well-funded public and cooperative systems of healthcare, including preventative care; holistic health with emphasis given to healthy environments and healthy and affordable food; and measures to reduce inequalities, a major source of vulnerability to health and other hazards.

Reduce Working Hours

Productivity has soared over the past century, as technical, informational, and organizational innovations alongside the use of fossil fuels multiplied the output of each human hour worked. Today, North American and Western European societies produce much more than enough for everyone (although maldistribution prevents a portion of citizens from fulfilling basic needs). This excess production begets desperate efforts to generate more demand by expanding markets, changing styles, and planning obsolescence. Breaking free of the growth imperative allows societies to adopt more appealing responses to overproduction: reduce the hours worked for market production and promote self-regulated community initiatives.

Automation and artificial intelligence need not lead to job losses. Reducing the weekly work hours of people already employed opens up more opportunities for people seeking employment. This move mitigates stress and anxiety on two fronts: exhaustion among those who work too much, and insecurity among those who have too little work.

Historically, with successive increases in productivity, mobilized workers have periodically achieved increases in wages and reductions in working hours. Structural changes implemented in recent decades, however, have redirected most productivity gains to company profits and shareholder dividends, while in many countries average wages have stagnated, and average working hours increased. Government and corporate policies can reverse this trend, reducing working hours through longer paid vacations, parental and family-care leave, sabbaticals, shorter daily hours, four-day work weeks, or facilitation of part-time work.[13] Legal safeguards and monitoring can support humane limits in service and remote jobs. In the US, for example, the rhythms of commercial truck driving changed significantly after the Federal Motor Carrier Safety Administration limited consecutive driving hours and instituted required breaks, all monitored electronically through vehicle computers.[14]

Reduction of fossil fuels, fertilizers, and other environment-damaging inputs will cause productivity to fall in some areas, meaning that more hours of work will be needed to produce the same goods. This is where the degrowth goals of decreasing production and consumption come together with energy transition, fair employment, and human–environmental wellbeing. Cutting total working hours reduces environmental impacts, including carbon emissions.[15] The less we work, the less we produce and consume, and the more time we have for non-monetized activities – including leisure, caring, and community engagement – that help to establish healthy and resilient societies.

Concerns that people would spend their additional free time shopping, taking exotic holidays, playing computer games, or otherwise using more energy and resources, underestimate how imaginative and resourceful people can be when they have the time and energy to think and create, as many of us did when we were children. The application of carbon fees can reduce the attraction of high-impact recreation industries, while public festivals and sports events can build cultural conditions for enjoying time with others.

Public Finance That Greens and Equalizes

How can the policies discussed here be funded without economic growth? A shift of political priorities away from increasing profits and GDPs opens up many options for reorganizing government revenues and expenditures.

Carbon fee and dividend programs, like those already operating in Canada and Switzerland, work simultaneously to reduce greenhouse gas emissions and generate shared income.[16] Analysts estimate that fees around $100 per ton would have effective impacts in the United States.[17] "Climate income" generated from such fees could be shared through public programs such as funding the universal basics described above, and/or returned to individuals through credits. Some proposals balance fees and dividends in ways that levy more carbon costs on high earners and increase the net income of people in the lower half of income distribution.

Successful implementation of carbon fees will lead to less carbon emissions, which is good for the planet, but also yield less cash dividends over time as carbon emissions decline. That foreseeable decline can be offset by scheduled increases in fees per unit, and by gradual shifts in priorities for government expenditures. Simply ending subsidies for fossil fuel exploration and exploitation will liberate significant resources. As citizens and politicians increasingly question expenditures allocated with the underlying intention of driving GDP growth (e.g. corporate subsidies, pharmaceutical development, or defense spending – which in the US totaled around $700 billion in 2019),[18] governments may redirect expenditures to their most valuable resource: healthy, happy human beings.

We need to stop taxing what sustains societies (people's work), and instead tax what destroys societies (pollution and inequality). Strategic taxes may be levied on water and air pollution, toxic wastes and emissions, or resource extraction. Taxes can help to moderate consumption of products unhealthy for the planet or its people: meat, sugary soft drinks, plastics, frequent flying. And whereas VAT and sales taxes can be regressive, luxury taxes (e.g. on SUVs, yachts, private jets) may serve as sources of revenue, gestures of fairness, and means to discourage conspicuous consumption and resource use.

Inequality can be mitigated via globally coordinated progressive taxes on wealth, like those Thomas Piketty proposes should be levied on capital, large inheritances, and estates, together with a global tax on financial transactions and translational profits.[19] Key also are progressive income taxes, like those introduced by the original New Deal, which helped to shape a period of unusual economic equality and intergenerational mobility in the US. Between 1936 and 1980, the highest marginal personal income tax rates for US residents ranged between 70 percent and 91 percent.[20] Today, such taxes will need international restrictions on fiscal paradises and tax havens to avoid a race to the bottom among countries using low tax rates to attract billionaires.[21]

Another suite of policies enabling fairer distribution of income include higher minimum and average wages, and rights of workers to organize and bargain. Perhaps even more vital are constraints on maximum earnings established by limits or steeply progressive taxes, promoting a common sense of "enough is enough."[22] An international standard called Wagemark is already used by companies, non-profit organizations, and government agencies to certify that the ratio between their highest and lowest earners is within 8:1.[23] And in 2016, the city of Portland, Oregon, voted to implement high surcharges on companies exceeding set ratios.[24]

If these taxes and limits are successful, economies will become more equitable and harms that are taxed will diminish – all good for societies and environments. At the same time, of course, revenues from these taxes may decline, changing balances of public finance. Longer-term plans may reduce expenditures on public services by reducing out-sourcing to for-profit enterprises, and focusing on low-cost interventions with high wellbeing returns (e.g. preventative healthcare with family doctors instead of the latest and most expensive hospital equipment). A gradual strengthening of lower-cost solidarity and community economies will be crucial to building low-impact low-cost worlds that are not experienced as painful austerity, but as common wellbeing.

Synergies

These five policy packages work together in synergy. Realignment of expenditures, together with corporate and wealth taxes, may fund Green New Deal measures or basic services. While basic incomes or carbon dividends might stimulate consumption among some people, resource taxes and carbon fees could disincentivize ecologically harmful choices. Policies that strengthen community economies provide outlets for creative energies liberated by reduced work hours or secured by a Universal Care Income. In the US, where the possibility of working less hours is constrained by policies that require full-time employment to access benefits such as healthcare, retirement, or education, universal basic services would free up businesses, schools, and others to hire and organize work in more fruitful ways.

Countless other policy changes that could contribute to positive degrowth transitions are not examined here due to constraints of space. Fundamental among these are proposals for changing money systems by limiting the domain of general purpose money, creating positive (or public) money, forbidding private banks to create new money through loans, and supporting community currencies and time-banks.[25] Also basic are policies for the transformation of food systems to reduce waste, transitions away from meat-heavy diets, and the promotion of agroecology and community-supported agriculture. Reviving and repopulating the countryside, reinvigorating rural economies and ecologies, can also be vital for supporting healthy degrowth.

Shared Planet, Different Realities

The proposals outlined here apply to OECD countries like Spain or the US, which we know well. Some may be fruitfully adapted to other contexts.

However, rather than projecting our own experiences onto non-Western or low-income countries, we are more interested in learning from proposals coming from their communities, civic societies, and environmental and social justice groups.

Degrowth makes a case for the OECD to put its own house in order before offering directions to the rest of the world, on whose backs it grew. A priority should be stopping the flow of money and natural resources from low- to high-income countries. As Jason Hickel reports, 2.5 times the amount of aid received by developing countries in 2012 was reappropriated by donor countries in the same year through debt payments and capital flight.[26] Equally substantial, though more difficult to quantify, are subsidies in the form of human resources provided by low-income societies who raise, educate, and care for humans who then serve as cheap labor for corporate interests, or migrate to work in high-income societies. To limit the flow of value toward wealthy countries, Hickel proposes closing down secrecy jurisdictions, penalizing bankers and accountants who facilitate illicit outflows, and imposing global taxes on corporate incomes to eliminate incentives for shifting money around the world. He joins many others in the call to write off the excess debts of poor countries, among other justifications as compensation for the ecological and carbon debts owed to them by high-income countries.[27]

Moves toward global environmental justice start with working against climate breakdown. Reduced production and consumption will lead to reduced emissions. However, the degrowth fight against climate change does not rest with shrinking GDPs. Interactions among the proposals outlined here are vital: investments in GNDs that mobilize energy transitions and restore ecosystems that absorb carbon; guarantees of low-carbon public services to all; carbon fees and dividends; reduced working hours that reduce emissions; and support for low-carbon community economies and lifestyles.

Related degrowth-minded proposals include a moratorium on new fossil fuel development; a ban of fossil fuel advertising; the phase-out of fossil fuel production, with just transition for workers in dependent industries; frequent flier levies; embargoes on any expansion of road networks and airports; policies for car-free cities; tight emissions standards for new cars and power stations; passive-house standards for new houses; and efficiency standards for rented properties.

In addition to curbing negative environmental impacts, the policies provided here also establish conditions for responding to an economic recession, where the objective from a degrowth perspective is not to re-launch growth, but to sustain wellbeing in the absence of growth. A GND can stimulate and shift employment to healthy parts of the economy that need development. Work-sharing can share diminishing employment among more workers. A Universal Care Income is vital for supporting people and letting them take care of themselves and dependents during economic dislocation, as well as floods, fires, storms, epidemics, and other forms of disaster that are intensifying with climate change. The significant decrease in oil prices during the pandemic crisis makes it a good moment to implement a carbon tax.

Many policies known to reduce carbon emissions and other forms of environmental damage, as well as policies known to strengthen health or care commons, are thwarted by fears that they will slow down economies. To avoid sacrificing the world's environmental and human health at the altar of growth, we seek to secure wellbeing and welfare without growth via the five path-breaking policy packages outlined in this chapter. Implementing these reforms is a tall order, and even taller in envisioned contexts of contraction, not stimulus and growth. Who will organize to see such a radical agenda through, and how? Who will be allies in this effort? What are the opportunities and barriers in current political environments? To these and other strategic questions we now turn.

5

Strategies for Mobilization

Envisaging the future is important. Equally important is organizing movement from here to there. In this chapter we ask how degrowth-oriented transformations can be mobilized, by whom, and for whom. We explore openings and obstacles among a wave of cultural changes, socioeconomic and climate crises, civil society unrest, and political party dynamics. We then look at opportunities and challenges for building alliances among a range of actors, interests, and movements that might lead to various forms of mobilization.

Erik Olin Wright talks of three strategies for transformation: interstitial (building alternatives in the cracks of current systems), symbiotic (working within systems for reforms), and ruptural (disrupting or revolting against dominant systems).[1] As we saw in Chapter 3, building interstitial alternatives is crucial to reducing dependence on economic growth and to performing everyday practices that shift common senses. We see promise in cooperatives, eco-communes, and other arrangements, which we do not conceive as exits from the system, but as purposeful practices that build common senses and political horizons oriented toward larger change. Systemic reforms like those described in Chapter 4 change the playing field to enable more people to make sense of needed changes, to live differently, and to contribute toward desired societies. Non-violent actions, protests, uprisings, strikes, and other forms of ruptural conflict also play necessary roles in defending initiatives and advocating further reforms.

Our strategy, therefore, is a coevolutionary one that articulates personal, communitarian, and political action and innovation. To realize policies and sustain politics, you need a strong base of people for whom degrowth is not an abstract idea but what they do every day. So our strategy starts with supporting community economies that nourish the grassroots and strengthen identities and common senses for the long game of building and sustaining low-impact worlds.

While degrowth futures move away from class, racial, gender, and colonial hierarchies that evolved to support growth, they neither privilege nor exclude certain groups. Political subjects are formed though practice and conflicts, as they support community economies and practice common senses that prefigure alternatives for prosperity without growth.

Faced with accelerating climate breakdown, inequalities, and authoritarianism, the pace of culture change proposed here may seem unduly slow. Of course we must also enact urgent responses. However, even with a gradual and cumulative process, tangible outcomes do not have to be slow. Unpredictable events can create new conditions, open or close possibilities, and shine new light on what is most fundamental for sustaining societies. Cultural adaptation can reach tipping points, after which change is fast and disruptive. Some studies find that it takes 25 percent of a population to catalyze social change.[2] Politics, Hannah Arendt has taught us, initiates the unexpected, the unprecedented. Within a few months, a solo "school strike for the climate" by a Swedish girl led to nationwide, then global, mobilizations that have impacted public opinion, political forums, and daily choices for a growing number of young (and not-so-young) people.

The Case for Degrowth

Openings Amid Consequences of Growth

Wright emphasizes the potential for social movements to seize opportunities amid unintended consequences of existing social orders. Climate crises open up extraordinary opportunities for mobilization around GNDs, carbon fees and dividends, and lifestyle changes. A majority of people in the UK, including almost half of Conservative voters, supports a radical program for a zero-carbon economy by 2030.[3] Loss of employment due to changing technologies, or to health or climate crises, creates opportunities for demanding a basic care income or reductions in work hours, while devastating inequality and poverty raise the possibility of considering wealth taxes, salary ratios, and universal services. And the accumulation of consumer, mortgage, and student debts, as well as national debts, renders systems vulnerable to organized strikes against debt payments.

Cultural changes also open up possibilities. For decades, environmental movements have been advocating lifestyle changes, but suggestions that car-driving and meat-eating pose problems for human and environmental health were dismissed as fringe notions of hippies and radical green parties. Today, however, moving around by bicycle, engaging in sharing economies, and eating plant-based diets have become such common sense that even McDonald's serves Beyond Meat Burgers. Whereas commercial and social media continue to promote competitive conspicuous consumption, these platforms are increasingly punctuated by worries about the sacrifices demanded by growth, concerning not only environmental damages, but also personal costs in the form of obsessions with money and appearance, debt, insecurities, loneliness, eating disorders, and addictions.

People around the world are searching for better ways of living and consuming: 70 percent of people surveyed in twenty-nine countries believe that overconsumption is putting our planet and society at risk, half say they could happily live without most of what they own, and respondents report that sharing everything from cars to textbooks and vacation homes has become commonplace.[4] Such shifts in culture and common senses do not translate automatically into consistent personal practices or voting behaviors. But they do establish fertile ground.

What trends in civil societies create possibilities for exerting pressure on governments to support this agenda? Starting in 2010, a series of protests and uprisings known collectively as the Arab

Spring, concurrent with Occupy Wall Street and the Spanish Indignados, expressed dissatisfaction with existing regimes in demands ranging from calls for incumbent governments to make policy changes to attempts to bring down entire political systems. Local outcomes varied from structural changes to brutal repression. Nearly a decade later, there is no clear consensus about the connections between and the historical causes of these protests. Among other issues, we perceive underlying troubles with growth, including dynamics of inequality, exploitation, and rollercoaster rides of growth and stagnation.

As we wrote this book in late 2019, massive protests were erupting in Chile, Ecuador, Haiti, Venezuela, Lebanon, and France, among other places. What direction will they take? While there is no single direct cause, and none waves the banner of degrowth, we again perceive troubles in political economies that are demanding increasing sacrifices and breaching increasingly dangerous limits in pursuit of growth. Political turbulence across Latin America, for example, is emerging amid experiences of debt and stagnation, following a decade in which growth had been fueled by surges of commodity extractivism (e.g. petroleum, mining, timber, soy), and governments had justified sacrifices made for this growth with promises of greater opportunity and prosperity for all.

As degrowth-supporting practices and ideas circulate and take root in everyday culture and civil society, conditions ripen for their expressions in official politics. Ideas that are talked about and desired among constituents are taken up and advanced by some political parties, and attacked by others.

The general proposal of degrowth has been debated in EU commissions and the UK House of Commons,[5] while aspects of the agenda are advanced in diverse political arenas. New Zealand's ruling Labour Party, for example, made an explicit move to prioritize wellbeing over GDP growth, and consequently designed its budget around bolstering mental and physical health, reducing child poverty, supporting indigenous peoples, moving to a low-carbon-emission economy, and flourishing in a digital age.[6] The UK Labour Party advocated a GND and UBS, a four-day working week, and the possibility of regulating, or wholly or partly nationalizing, power sectors, railways, and other public infrastructure with the intention of weaning them off fossil fuels.[7] In the heart of the COVID-19 pandemic, the Spanish Parliament is drafting plans for a minimum income guaranteed for those in need.

Nevertheless, growth is still at the center of most

official politics. New Zealand's Labour Party may no longer officially embrace GDP, but it is overseeing an economy growing at 2 percent each year. We have not heard any elected political leader explicitly advocate degrowth, a risky move in corporate-dependent media and political environments. Those who support our path-breaking reforms often construe them as compatible with economic growth. With time, however, and through the arduous work of grassroots change, we expect that cultural, economic, and environmental pressures will induce some politicians and parties to de-articulate the transformative policies and visions they already support from the conventional expectations of growth to which they cling.

Challenges Amid Consequences of Growth

Backlash against the ideas proposed here is rallied in the name of stability, defense of geopolitical interests, and traditional identities. The conservative philosopher John Gray affirms that "the project of promoting maximal economic growth is perhaps the most vulgar ideal ever put before a suffering humankind."[8] But he also warns that a political project that reduces material consumption for large numbers of people will face a "populist backlash and geopolitical upheaval [that] will derail any transition to a stationary state."[9]

The end of growth poses serious threats to stability in political economies built around growth. Citizens who suffer pain and disruption wrought by unbidden stagnation, recession, and austerity understandably reject calls to halt growth voluntarily. Some politicians find it expedient to deny evidence of troubles with growth, and to attack messengers who draw attention to those signs. As detailed in Chapter 2, in these unstable times, governments have doubled down on growth to distract citizens from the need for redistribution, to prop up outdated forms of employment in changing productive systems, and to fund welfare services. In times of economic crisis, when growth falters, attacks on degrowth visions and calls for a return to the normality of growth often become more aggressive.

Economic growth buttresses geopolitical power. From colonial expansion to Cold War arms races, national growth has been closely tied to strength in the global forum. Superior economic power allows some countries to cheaply access and exploit human and natural resources in others, while resulting revenues enable huge military investments, employed to create and defend those opportunities.

What conditions could open up opportunities for a pacific retreat in which reduced consumption and greater domestic sufficiency in energy and food free OECD countries from the need to colonize and exploit others? Multi-scale strategies are needed to integrate the localization of some processes with a strengthening of the mechanisms of international governance, such as the UN, the EU, and the IPCC, a call which goes beyond a degrowth agenda alone. Without global coordination and enforcement, proposals like a GND or a wealth tax levied in one country could provoke a flight of foreign and domestic capital, turning organized transition to a steady state into a disordered collapse. Cooperation among countries can complement and support domestic prioritization of solidary provisioning to enhance autonomy from foreseen turbulence in global processes.

Emerging synergies between authoritarian and reactionary impulses spell trouble. Historical experience shows that sudden economic downturns can nourish authoritarian forces, who garner power with messages that blame target groups for declines, and promise a return to previous prosperity and order. Changing conditions require changing responses; both generate anxiety. Politicians can exacerbate fear of change by encouraging constituents to feel that their identities, values, and lifeways are threatened by proposed responses. Recent examples include successful far-right and white nationalist campaigns to nurture climate and pandemic denialism, anti-feminism, anti-abortion, anti-environmentalism, anti-vegetarianism, anti-migration, and similar postures.

It will be difficult for those mobilizing degrowth to make headway in electoral politics, to compromise with drives for geopolitical domination, and to endure violent backlash and reactionary authoritarianism. The explosion of civil disobedience summarized above points to some options, notably the exercise of massive non-violent protest to contest those who use violence to maintain undemocratic and untenable orders. Yet, the fear of various forms of economic, social, and political disorder that may erupt in the absence of growth is one of the biggest deterrents for citizens and politicians who are otherwise sympathetic to the values and proposals advanced here.

Alliance-Building

In this daunting political environment, alliances are fundamental. Millions of potential allies can be found among nature-lovers, care-providers, families with children, biking fanatics, vegans, overworked professionals, hippies, unemployed people, indebted families, climate refugees, back-to-the-landers, senior citizens, people engaged in anti-colonial and anti-capitalist movements, and more. Here we look at a few among many vital allies: workers, feminists, anti-racists, and members of low-income communities.

People working in manufacturing, construction, transportation, schools, hospitals, hospitality, groceries, and other sectors are indispensable allies, and worker organizations ranging from conventional trade unions to online communities are central to mobilization. However, proposals to end our reliance on fossil fuels and curb ecological damage have been portrayed as enemies of workers' demands for jobs, standards of living, and security. Basic incomes and other policies can help transcend this perceived antagonism between jobs and the environment, while patient and persistent listening and conversation will be necessary to collaboratively develop degrowth visions and language that resonate with workers. That investment is vital for creating spaces for working-class environmentalisms and supporting a just, worker-centered transition.

In contexts where mega-corporations controlling

crucial means of production impede moves toward equitable low-carbon futures, production is a core site of struggle. Through contract demands, strikes, blockades, and other actions, organized workers can exercise their power to disrupt the production processes on which global metabolic flows depend. In these struggles, workers are no longer alone. As David Harvey notes, struggles over the environment, over desires and ways of living, and over care and reproduction are fundamentally about modes of production, and therefore relevant to struggles over conditions of labor.[10] Alliances for change that make sense for workers, rather than threaten them, may be built around the goals of dignified work, equitable salary distribution, free time, universal care, and access to housing and food, among others.

Concerns addressed in this book are informed by and align with those of feminists who have led public mobilization and intellectual critique around work, including non-commodified and sub-market care work for homes, health, nourishment, children, and sick and elderly people. Feminists have heightened our awareness of the gendered sacrifices inherent in economic systems that demand full-time labor from all adults, putting the squeeze on work through which human lives, communities, and environments are reproduced day by day and over generations. Actors and organizations concerned with salary inequities along gender and ethnoracial lines may ally with our proposals for maximum, minimum, and caring incomes.

Alliances with actors and movements working against racism are challenging and vital dimensions of this mission. In mainstream environmentalism, white men have dominated organizational leadership, science, and media. Even within climate action movements, students and grassroots members experience currents of racialization, patriarchy, and coloniality that make it difficult to work together equitably.[11] Hierarchical dualisms linked together in Western culture (humans/nature, white/non-white, men/women, heteronormative/queer) make it difficult for environmentalists who embody dominant identities to challenge the status quo – even the human exceptionalism that justifies the domination and exploitation of non-human nature.

In contrast, grassroots environmental and social justice movements in low-income and wealthy countries alike have frequently been inspired, led, and publicly represented by actors who are not men, not white, and not wealthy. Not incidentally, they have advanced more radical proposals, such as Martin Luther King Jr.'s 1967 call for a guaranteed basic income to abolish poverty and decrease inequality, or the Zapatistas' demand for autonomous spaces to create a future outside of Mexico's national development. In order to learn from and build alliances with anti-racist and diversely positioned social justice movements, degrowth advocates must prioritize mutual and respectful dialogue among diverse knowledges and ways of knowing.

Why would billions of people living in low-income communities and countries support a movement that seems to hinder hopes of enjoying some of the promised benefits of economic growth? First, we must recognize the extremely different conditions and positions among these populations. To many living on frontiers of global expansion, the contraction of European or North American economies can bring relief. Indigenous communities we have worked with in Brazil, Bolivia, Mexico, and Ecuador risk their lives fighting against incursions of mining, logging, drilling, roads, and agribusiness, in defense of long-evolving solidarity and kin economies.

Degrowth may seem less appealing to urban middle classes and political leaders in Latin America, Africa, and elsewhere, who are trying to improve standards of living and pay off debts with the pittances they obtain from extractivist concessions, taxes on multinational corporations, and similar.

Not to mention China, where generations who had suffered deprivation are now caught up in economic and material growth at scales unprecedented in human history.

Our case illuminates ways in which the drive for growth has shaped colonialism, sexism, racism, and other inequities; but we do not argue that our proposals for degrowth are relevant for all actors positioned in the resulting uneven terrains. Operating from positions in wealthy northern societies, we seek to learn with and from others. Drawing on feminist and decolonial approaches to support mobilization less influenced by historical hierarchies, Dengler and Seebacher argue that "degrowth is not to be misunderstood as proposal from the Global North imposed on the Global South, but rather a Northern supplement to Southern concepts, movements and lines of thought. It is therefore imperative for degrowth to seek alliances with these Southern 'fellow travelers.'"[12] Arturo Escobar identifies points of convergence among moves toward degrowth in the north and toward post-development in Latin America: originating from different intellectual traditions and operating through different epistemic and political practices, they combine radical questioning of core assumptions of growth and economism with visions of alternative worlds based on ecological integrity and social justice.[13]

Those in other parts of the world who are fighting on their own terms for meaningful, equitable, and ecologically sustainable worlds should know that we are engaged in a parallel fight, in the belly of the beast. Even sincere commitments to dialogue and alliance across these differences meet obstacles.[14] In interviews with environmental justice activists, Beatriz Rodríguez-Labajos and colleagues found that "In parts of Africa, Latin America and many other regions of the Global South, including poor and marginalised communities in Northern countries, the term degrowth is not appealing, and does not match people's demands."[15] Susan Paulson has identified rewards, as well as challenges, of dialogue across difference during a multi-year collaboration among researchers from varied cultural, linguistic, and national backgrounds learning from communities around the world who prioritize wellbeing and solidarity, rather than increased production and consumption.[16] In our experience, common senses of degrowth, rather than the word itself, do resonate with people living in diverse low-income contexts.

In sum, degrowth visions and proposals draw from and take root among ideas and practices of people in many positions, including long-established religious or spiritual beliefs and everyday life in low-income communities. Rather than replace traditions of worker's struggles or modern development with a new universalizing path, we learn from allies like the Global Tapestry of Alternatives to support conditions in which a plurality of pathways can thrive in mutual respect, reflecting the Zapatista dream of "a world where many worlds fit."[17]

Mobilizing for Political Change

What forms of mobilization and political action will emerge from connections among such diverse positions and interests? We recognize that aspects of degrowth politics may alienate or complicate some interests of elected officials, workers, low-income communities, and others. Climate scientists and activists, for example, furiously debate the costs and benefits of alliances with proposals like degrowth. US scientist Michael Mann fears that linking climate movements to more radical proposals "risks alienating needed supporters (say, independents and moderate conservatives) who are apprehensive about a broader agenda of progressive social change."[18]

Strategies for Mobilization

Acknowledgement that degrowth is unlikely to become a banner of massive mobilizations uniting many movements invites a search for other metaphors for political organizing. Padini Nirmal and Dianne Rocheleau suggest learning from networks, roots, and rhizomes that constitute both ends and means in many struggles to defend diverse nature-cultures, especially among indigenous and marginalized people.[19] Plants like bamboo and poison ivy reproduce and expand via rhizomes, also known as rootstocks, in which horizontal networks of stems at or under the soil surface develop nodes where new roots and new shoots extend vertically.

Indeed, degrowth visions, ideas, and actions are already being harbored and circulated through subterranean networks of relationships that interconnect and nourish cultural, civic, and political allies. In response to contingent opportunities, we expect to see those webs develop more nourishing roots, and give rise to more visible shoots that enact desired changes. We look forward to seeing new shoots erupt in electoral campaigns and massive non-violent protests, as well as rainbows of unexpected expressions. This type of mobilization is hard to eradicate. Even when visible ventures meet setbacks and backlash, pieces of rhizome – in this case, degrowth common senses, practices, and relationships – are left behind in the soil where they grow and emerge in new manifestations.

Exercising, Legislating, and Mobilizing Desired Worlds, Day by Day

Earlier in this book, we observed that it is easier to imagine the end of the world, even the end of capitalism, than the end of growth. Even when economies falter or plummet, the desire for and pursuit of growth can intensify. It can seem equally difficult to mobilize political action toward degrowth. Nevertheless, in relation to other scenarios on the horizon, we are convinced that degrowth is a more humane and equitable path forward. And we are encouraged by instances in which degrowth common senses, practices, and politics are already being mobilized as people come together to produce, consume, and live differently, recuperating old and generating new modes of (re)production and social organization. We recognize that the journey will not be straightforward or uncomplicated, but contradictory, with setbacks, counter-reforms, repressions, readjustments, and unexpected turns.

Throughout the book we have used examples

from Barcelona to emphasize the articulation among community economies, political mobilization, and institutional reform. With roots in the occupied plazas of 2011, and mobilized by activists seasoned in the city's deep-rooted cooperative economies, the Barcelona in Common party was formed in 2014 from the bottom-up through open assemblies. Alliances were forged among working-class constituents suffering the effects of economic and housing crises and young or mid-life people living in, or in the periphery of, Barcelona's vibrant community economies and social justice struggles. Within a year of its founding, and in an accelerated turn of events, the party won the municipal elections. In parallel processes elsewhere, the Occupy movement evolved into Momentum, a political organization that radicalized some policy commitments of the UK Labour Party, while the Sunrise movement and democratic socialists in the US energized Bernie Sanders' campaign.

The political effectiveness and sustainability of these movements remains to be seen. (Geo)political changes, national dividing lines, and context-specific dynamics can thwart even the best of projects. But what we want you to keep from the Barcelona case, and what might be relevant for similar experiences of political parties emerging through or reshaped by social movements, is the articulation of alliances across difference amid deep-rooted and embodied cultural change.

You still might not be convinced that a politics of degrowth is feasible. We have our doubts too. We understand the political risks of instability in stagnant economies and the challenges of developing political projects under conditions of contraction, not expansion. Many who share degrowth values and visions, but perceive degrowth as politically impossible, promote a politics premised on making growth green and inclusive. However, as we argued in Chapter 2, and further demonstrate in the following Frequently Asked Questions, a green, inclusive growth simply does not seem feasible or desirable. There is no technological or policy fix that can generalize to nine billion people the material standard of living currently enjoyed by a minority at high cost to others. That means that either institutions of sharing toward equitable wellbeing will be developed and expanded, or else large parts of the global population will be expulsed as expedient surplus.

The most immediate case for degrowth that we try to communicate in this book is that a modest life based on cooperation and sharing is desirable in and of itself. Even if endless growth were economically, socially, and ecologically sustainable, it would still not bring the fullness of human life that we seek. The case for degrowth is not about martyred self-denial or constraining human potential; it is about reorienting socioeconomies to support collaborative and creative construction of lives that are pleasurable, healthy, satisfying, and sustainable for more people and more places. End goals of degrowth – dignified work, less selfish competition, more equitable relationships, identities not ranked by individual achievement, solidary communities, humane rhythms of life, respect for natural environments – are also the means through which people exercise and embody, day by day, the lifestyles, institutions, and politics of degrowth worlds to come.

Frequently Asked Questions

Green Growth

(1) *Aren't economies damaging the environment less as they grow richer?*
No, they are not. Rich economies use more resources and emit more carbon (per capita) than poor ones. The economies of wealthier countries might impact the environment less *per unit* of GDP; but they produce more total GDP per capita, using more resources and emitting more waste per capita. The "Environmental Kuznets hypothesis" according to which countries damage the environment more as they develop, reaching a certain point of wealth at which economic growth becomes less damaging, has been soundly discredited with statistical data.[1] Some mid-income countries adopt environmental standards earlier than wealthier ones. For big prob-

lems like carbon emissions, there is no inversion of trends at higher incomes: the richer a country gets, the more CO_2 it emits. Moreover, high-income countries shift their environmental costs to poorer countries by importing resources and industrial goods, and by exporting waste.

(2) *Can't we produce more with less?*
We can. But GDPs cannot continue growing while using fewer and fewer resources.[2] From 1980 to 2002, global material flows grew 1.78 percent each year, slower than global GDP, but growing nonetheless. From 2002 to 2013 material flows grew 3.85 percent per year, faster than global GDP. Today, a 1 percent difference in GDP between economies corresponds to 0.8 percent difference in material use.[3] Domestic resource use in some high-income economies, like the US, seems to have peaked and declined, but this is because inputs are outsourced through globalization. If one calculates the amount of materials used to produce the goods and services consumed in the US, including imports, then its material footprint has grown in step with GDP (same for the EU and the OECD).[4] Granted, the future does not have to be like the past. But all models predict a significant increase in global material use by 2050. Even under the most stringent

technology and policy assumptions, resource use will increase 17 percent.[5]

(3) Can't resources be used more efficiently?

They can. In growth economies, however, the more efficiently resources are used, the cheaper they become, and the more total resources get used.[6] This is the essence of economic growth: labor and resource productivity free resources that are then devoted to more production and new services, extracting more value. Efficiency gains from specific appliances or conservation measures may not fully backfire. However, the more resource-efficient economies are also those with bigger material use. Don't get us wrong, resource efficiency is important; but we call for efficiently doing less with less, rather than doing more with less, because more means more damage. A good way to move there is to combine efficiency improvements with limits: caps or mandated reductions in resources or pollutants.

The rabbit of the efficiency hat also cannot be pulled out indefinitely – there is an upper boundary of energy/resource efficiency, beyond which further growth will lead to more energy (resource) use. There are limits not only on how far, but also on how fast efficiency can improve. The energy efficiency of some goods like refrigerators or cars has been increasing at 2 percent per year over the last thirty-five years (close to the average rate of growth), but not everything can improve so quickly. Air travel efficiency hasn't changed much, and power plants improved only 1 percent per year.[7]

(4) *Can't clean resources substitute for polluting ones?*

Yes, they can, but cleaner substitutes also pollute, and if the economy grows, so will their use and pollution. Solar and wind are cleaner than coal, but the energy they generate is stored on batteries using lithium or cobalt. Using these cleaner technologies, world demand for rare-earth elements – and Earth-destroying mining and refining – need to rise 300 to 1,000 percent by 2050 just to meet the Paris climate agreement's goals.[8] The real goal moreover is decreasing dirty alternatives (fossil fuels, gas-guzzling cars, etc.), not just adding new ones. Sales of electric vehicles are growing, but so are sales of SUVs. Solar and wind power are growing quickly, but they have not yet reduced fossil fuel use, only added more energy to the system.[9] Increasing cleaner substitutes is necessary but not sufficient.

(5) *Isn't it just a matter of getting the prices right?*
Polluters should pay for polluting, yes. But there is no "right price" determined by the market.[10] Resources and carbon should be taxed at levels sufficiently high for the reductions needed. Taxing a ton of carbon at anything from $100 to $5,000 by 2030 compared to just $8 today (the high range of a tax some scientists deem necessary for stopping climate change) would practically prohibit oil and coal. This could slow down the economy, which is fine. But this is also why the powers that be do not allow it to happen. Growth rests on cheapness. The problem is that if polluters have to pay too much, polluting industries will use their political and economic power to try to stop the charges. So the challenge is less about getting the markets or the prices right, as about leveraging the political power to do so.

(6) *Can't we have growth based only on information and ideas?*
In science fiction, yes, in reality no. We can imagine a movie where people sleep, plugged into a grid and fed by robots, exchanging more and more money in their dream world without using more resources (although this arrangement would not use less, either). In the real world, however, the monu-

114

mental growth of information and communicati̲
technologies (ICTs) has not reduced resource use.
Countries with more developed ICTs have bigger
material footprints. As economies move from
agriculture to industry to services, their material
footprints grow rather than shrink. ICT services are
resource- and energy-intensive (think of the power
running servers), and those making money selling
information or communication use money to buy or
invest in material goods (think of the private jets of
internet entrepreneurs).

(7) *Why degrowth, and not just circular economy?*
Turning today's overdeveloped economies circular
is not sufficient. Because economies are entropic, it
takes energy and resources, human and natural, to
recycle and reuse stuff or to use renewable energy.[11]
The bigger the circle is and the faster the circulation, the more energy and resources used. Industrial
revolution was a great linearization. Returning to
circular, renewable flows of energy and materials
will, more than likely, slow down current economies
geared on cheap, linear extraction and disposal.[12]
So circular economy and degrowth can and will
advance together.

(8) *Aren't some countries already reducing carbon emissions while growing?*

Yes. Eighteen of the thirty-six OECD countries reduced emissions by 2.4 percent on average per year between 2005 and 2015. Accounting for imported goods does not change the basic pattern. Significant and welcome as these reductions may be, they fall far short of the fast decarbonization needed, which, according to some calculations, is 8–10 percent each year for high-income countries.[13] Reducing emissions is easier with less growth. If your economy grows by 3 percent annually, you have to cut emissions by around 6 percent relative to the size of the economy to achieve 3 percent cuts in emission per year. With 1 percent growth, this falls to 4 percent. Fighting climate change with economic growth is like running up a down escalator that is accelerating. Whether the global economy grows eleven times by the end of the century or stays steady makes a huge difference. Indeed, the eighteen countries that reduced their emissions grew much less than other countries (energy and GDP growing annually at around 1 percent, on average).[14]

(9) *Won't spending for a Green New Deal stimulate growth?*

Possibly yes in the short term. But if GNDs succeed in their goal of eliminating fossil fuels, it is doubtful that growing income from renewable energies would be sufficient to sustain growth. For every unit of energy you spend to produce solar and wind power you generally get less energy than you do from coal, oil, or natural gas.[15] Less net energy means less labor productivity. Less productivity means less growth. A Green New Deal can reduce carbon emissions, generate meaningful jobs, and pay for itself by the returns of the projects it funds. But it may also slow down the economy in the long run. We believe this is fine, as long as institutions are put in place to manage well without growth.

(10) *Why not just move beyond GDP?*

GDP measures what this economy depends upon, which is market growth. GDP was not designed to measure welfare, and does so poorly. It mixes goods with bads: an oil spill is good for the economy because money is spent on cleaning. And it does not account for unpaid services: if you marry your lawyer and she takes care of your affairs for free, GDP falls. New sets of wellbeing and prosperity measurements, such as the Genuine

Progress Indicator, can help show how growth is failing societies, and offer glimpses of new kinds of speedometers needed after the end of growth. But changing the speedometer of the car won't reduce the speed. You also need to change the vehicle: replace a growth-driven economy with degrowth.

(11) *Why not growth in wellbeing?*
Improvement in wellbeing is exactly what we call for, achieved with a reduction in use of resources and energy, and less environmental damage. That improvement is distinct from material and GDP growth.

(12) *Why not growth of good things and degrowth of bad ones?*
Yes, selective degrowth is what we advocate. Many good things we want (conservation of nature and resources, empowerment of marginalized people in extractive areas, fewer working hours) will slow down the GDP economy, which should be handled with foresight. Even good things (say solar panels) use bad things (rare metals), so the increase of some good things must be moderated. Finally, for many things we care about (public health, education, childcare) what we need are qualitative improve-

ments, not quantitative increase, so the vocabulary of growth here is misleading.

(13) *Do your small-scale solutions scale up?*
Some may, others will not. We call for *more* localized, community economies, not for *everything* to be produced small-scale or cooperatively. Decentralized, agroecological production requires more labor per unit of output compared to industrial agriculture, but also uses fewer chemicals and fossil fuels. Providing a greater percentage of a population's food with community-supported agriculture interacts with other adjustments, including reducing food waste, eating less meat, and eating more seasonal and regionally grown produce. Community modes will likely continue to be complemented by more centralized production of goods such as grains and minerals. Smaller-scale alternatives complement and increase resilience. Urban gardeners cannot cover all nutritional needs, but they can cultivate a substantial share of seasonal vegetables, which would otherwise be transported from far away by planes or ships. Urban food gardens, for example, saved Cuba from a possible famine when the economy collapsed after the fall of the Soviet Union.[16]

(14) *Is it possible to decrease energy use so much?*
It is plausible. The 2000-watt society vision of the Federal Institute of Technology in Zürich shows that average Western citizens could reduce their primary energy usage to 2,000 watts per year (the current global average) by the year 2050, without lowering their standard of living, mostly through interventions in mobility, buildings, and energy production. Researchers calculate that by combining sufficiency with efficiency measures, the typical electricity use of a two-person household in Germany could be lowered even more, by 75 percent, without drastic lifestyle changes.[17] The average American exceeds this six times and the average Swiss three, but an Indian consumes only one twelfth.[18]

Growth, Poverty, and Inequality

(15) *Isn't growth needed to fight poverty?*
Growth is insufficient for tackling poverty. Despite phenomenal growth in recent decades, there are 40 million poor in the US, and 11 million in the UK – 12 percent and 17 percent of the population respectively – the same share as in the 1970s. In 2008, 24 percent of people in high-income countries still lived with less than the socially acceptable

minimum in their country.[19] Growth is also not an effective mechanism for reducing global poverty. The poorest 60 percent of humanity receive only 5 percent of all new income generated by global growth. The fruits of growth could be distributed better, no doubt. But so could a steady, or declining output. Growth is used as the excuse to not redistribute, both because redistribution is thought to limit growth, and because growth conveys promises to improve everyone's condition in the future. In that sense, the pursuit of growth is an obstacle to tackling poverty.

(16) *Isn't growth necessary for reducing inequalities?*

At a global scale, inequality among all individuals has been declining due to rises in formerly very low incomes in China and South-East Asia. However, inequalities between countries and between individuals within countries have been increasing in recent decades despite economic growth. We used to think that increasing inequalities were a feature of early industrialization, and that as a country gets richer, inequality declines. But as Thomas Piketty has shown, the mid-twentieth-century reduction in income gaps was the result not of growth, but of the destruction of wealth during the Great Depression and World War II, followed by powerful egalitarian policies in Europe and North America. Since 1980, growth has come with more, not less, inequality.[20] Policy matters more than growth. Granted, tax revenue may increase with growth, allowing progressive governments to spend more for social purposes. But current taxes are much lower in the UK and the US than they were decades ago, when their economies produced a fraction of what they produce now. In contexts where growth serves as an excuse for elites to pay less, relative poverty has become a structural feature of contemporary economies, no matter how much they grow.

(17) *Does degrowth demand unrealistic reductions of people's income?*
It is undesirable, not to mention politically impossible, to demand a two-thirds decrease in median incomes in high-income countries in order to converge with the rest of the world. But here we have talked about decrease in resource and energy use, not directly in incomes. A two-thirds reduction in energy use is thinkable. The incomes of some people living a comfortable middle-class life may decline under degrowth, but absolute incomes don't tell us much about quality of life. Spain's GDP per capita in 1985 was almost half what it is now, but

Spaniards' standard of living was not noticeably worse. Spanish GDP per capita is 60 percent of the US's (and salaries are much lower), yet those of us in Barcelona live as well as those in Florida. The purchasing power of incomes depends on cost of living, and on whether basic goods are private or public, deregulated or regulated. Three of us in Europe have access to a public health system, while Susan in the US doesn't, so our lower European salaries are more affordable than would otherwise be the case.

(18) *Is degrowth against growth in poor countries?* Reducing Africa's material footprint is neither necessary nor desirable. But that doesn't mean that a Europe- or US-like growth society should be built there; people should be free to chart their own paths to wellbeing. Middle-income countries like Costa Rica achieve human development standards at a fraction of the income and resource use of rich countries.[21] Poor people need clean water, public healthcare, affordable housing, and food – not generalized GDP growth that often ends up in the foreign bank accounts of local elites.

(19) *Do rich countries have to grow to lift the rest of the world out of poverty?*

No, they don't. On the contrary, more growth by rich countries can only worsen the conditions of poorer societies ravaged by climate change and environmental disasters caused by growth. The energy required to satisfy basic needs in poor countries will consume a substantial share of the remaining global carbon budget.[22] So, high-consumption nations and people must degrow to free space for low-consumption ones. The West grew rich by exploiting the rest, so it is strange to claim now that it must keep growing out of charity in order to buy the products of the poor. Trickle down or development aid discourses make it seem as if growth in the West is helping develop the global South. Instead, high-income countries would do better to pay back some of their ecological debts, and reverse unequal capital and resource flows.

Managing Without Growth

(20) *Won't debts explode without growth?*

Possibly, but the economy cannot be forced to grow at the fictitious interest rates banks and financiers charge. International mechanisms must be instituted for debt forgiveness. Debt jubilees for low-income countries can compensate ecological and carbon debts, while established processes of democratic Debt Audits can help distinguish payable from odious debts. In the long term, lending institutions must change. Lending with interest makes growth necessary to pay back interest; this can be mitigated if lenders are not allowed to relend interest, or if they charge only a one-off fee for the service of lending, not a compound interest. How new money enters the economy could also change. Right now, money is produced as debt, through loans given by private banks. Instead, under public (positive) money proposals, the state could create money without debt, spending it for socially useful projects – say a GND or UBS.[23]

(21) *Won't unemployment increase without growth?*

No, not necessarily. Policies determine how employment interacts with growth. One percent lower growth in Japan or Austria leads to only 0.15 percent more unemployment, compared with 0.85 percent more in Spain.[24] Reducing the hours of each worker creates new jobs, and so does public spending on GNDs, UBS, or social care. If productivity declines because of a shift away from fossil fuels, then there will be more demand for human labor. If productivity increases because of automation, then reduced working hours can avoid unemployment.

(22) *Why don't you talk about reversing population growth?*

Population growth is an outcome of growth systems that need cheap labor and consumers; with degrowth we focus on causes, not symptoms. True, there's a strong correlation between higher GDP and lower fertility, but there is no evidence that fertility will start increasing if GDP declines. It is clear that education, health, and gender equality opportunities enjoyed by some high-income countries are being achieved by others at much lower GDPs. Empowering and defending women's education and rights to control their bodies, implementing public policies such as pensions and public health, and promoting cultural and lifestyle changes can all slow population growth, as they have in many parts of the world.[25]

(23) *Will peoples' wellbeing suffer without growth?*

It depends. Growth has ceased to improve objective or subjective wellbeing.[26] The global genuine progress index, a robust collection of wellbeing indicators, shows stagnation since the 1950s in some high-income countries, like the US, and since the 1960s, 1970s or 1980s in others. Only one in three US residents report themselves as being "very happy," a percentage that has fluctuated, but not changed significantly, since 1973, in spite of sky-rocketing GDP. Mid-income countries have similar life expectancies as high-income ones, and residents of some mid-income countries, like Costa Rica, report higher levels of satisfaction than high-income ones like the US or Hong Kong. Equality has a much stronger effect on society-wide wellbeing than GDP. And, as the Harvard Adult Development study found, the greatest predictor of individual wellbeing is not income or class, but social relations. Economic contractions may negatively impact wellbeing if they lead to certain austerity measures, but not if they lead to lifestyle changes with positive dietary and health effects, or if they bring people closer together. Degrowth is not simply a contraction of the economy, it is a project of living meaningfully, enjoying simple pleasures, sharing and relating more with others, and working less, in more equal societies. Degrowth could *improve* wellbeing.

You convinced me. But what can I do?

We can speak to one another and spread the story shared in this book. We can create circles, reading groups, open universities, schools, offline and online, to discuss what is to be done.[27]

We can spend more time in and resources on cooperative spaces of living, producing, and consuming outside the growth economy. That may involve joining consumer cooperatives, working for non-profit or public entities, investing savings in cooperative or ethical banks, buying from socially responsible providers, or growing fruits and vegetables in local gardens. As private and public systems falter and fail to satisfy our needs, we can come together to help one another cope, setting up new structures and renewing commons and public sectors.

We can shift our behaviors to reduce our carbon and material footprints: buy less and share more; reuse and recycle where possible; eat less meat; fly and drive less; use trains, public transport, and bicycles more; get electricity from renewable energy providers, ideally cooperatives.

We can vote for those who want to help advance initiatives like the ones presented here. We can warn our representatives that we won't vote for them unless they stop glorifying growth and instead commit to pushing the five-reforms agenda. We can help the politicians and political parties we support by contributing to their organizing and door-to-door campaigns.

We can join a trade or student union, if we haven't already, and strike for better conditions and shorter work hours. We could advocate responses to climate change. We can participate in protests and direct actions against austerity, evictions, rising university fees, and student debt, or for the right to the city, housing rights, or workers', women's, immigrants', or cleaners' rights. We can recognize that many of the struggles happening in our towns and workplaces are rooted in forces that push growth, while demanding a greater and greater sacrifice for growth.

Yes, a day with twenty-four hours is too short for all this. We have to make a living, in conditions that, in many contexts, are increasingly difficult. We also have the right to find joy in our lives, and with others, whether partying, making music, conversing, or protesting. We can be vulnerable and let others take care of us, in the knowledge that we will take care of them too. We can learn to live with our contradictions (up to seven, remember!). And finally, be kind with ourselves as we are with others.

Notes

1 A Case for Degrowth

1 D.H. Meadows, D.L. Meadows, J. Randers, and W. Behrens III, *The Limits to Growth*, New York: Universe Books, 1972; E.J. Mishan, *The Costs of Economic Growth*, London: Staples Press, 1967.

2 "Global Inequality," at https://inequality.org/facts/global-inequality.

3 United States Census Bureau, American Community Survey (ACS), 2018 Data Release New and Notable (2019), at https://www.census.gov/programs-surveys/acs/news/data-releases/2018/release.html.

4 Y. Varoufakis, Twitter post, 2018, at https://twitter.com/yanisvaroufakis/status/1042351984559513600.

5 W. Steffen et al., "Planetary Boundaries: Guiding Human Development on a Changing Planet," *Science* 347(6223), 2015: 1259855-1–10.

6 See W.J. Ripple, C. Wolf, T.M. Newsome, M. Galetti, M. Alamgir, E. Crist, M.I. Mahmoud, W.F.

Laurance, and 15,364 scientist signatories from 184 countries, "World Scientists' Warning to Humanity: A Second Notice," *BioScience* 67(12), 2017: 1026–8.

7 E. Hirsch, "The Unit of Resilience: Unbeckoned Degrowth and the Politics of (Post)development in Peru and the Maldives," *Journal of Political Ecology* 24, 2017: 462–75.

8 L. Berg, "Clean Water and the Environmental Justice Movement," Shared Justice (2019), at http://www.sharedjustice.org/domestic-justice/2019/6/12/clean-water-and-the-environmental-justice-movement.

9 ESRI ArcGIS Storymaps, Louisiana Cancer Alley, ArcGIS, at http://www.arcgis.com/apps/MapJournal/index.html?appid=ffeea5ac225040a380aa11b25e786a68.

10 R. Wilkinson and K. Pickett, *The Spirit Level: Why More Equal Societies Almost Always Do Better*, New York: Bloomsbury, 2011.

11 European Environment Bureau, *Decoupling Debunked – Evidence and Arguments Against Green Growth as a Sole Strategy for Sustainability*, Brussels: EEB, 2019.

12 S. Singh and W. Haas, "Aid, Metabolism, and Social Conflicts in the Nicobar Islands," in *Ecological Economics from the Ground Up*, New York: Routledge/Earthscan, 2012; J. Suzman, *Affluence without Abundance: The Disappearing World of the Bushmen*, New York: Bloomsbury, 2017.

13 UN Environment International Resource Panel, Global Material Flows Database, UN Environment,

at http://www.resourcepanel.org/global-material-fl ows-database.

14 Pope Francis, *Laudato si' of the Holy Father Francis on Care for our Common Home*, Vatican: Libreria Editrice Vaticana, 2015.

15 See M. Weiss and C. Cattaneo, "Degrowth: Taking Stock and Reviewing an Emerging Academic Paradigm," *Ecological Economics* 137, 2017: 220–30.

16 A. Kothari, A. Salleh, A. Escobar, F. Demaria, and A. Acosta, *Pluriverse: A Post-Development Dictionary*, New York: Columbia University Press, 2019; A. Kothari, F. Demaria, and A. Acosta, "Buen Vivir, Degrowth, and Ecological Swaraj: Alternatives to Sustainable Development and the Green Economy," *Development* 57(3–4), 2014: 362–75.

17 C. Dengler and L. Seebacher, "What About the Global South? Towards a Feminist Decolonial Degrowth Approach," *Ecological Economics* 157, 2019: 246–52; S. Paulson, "Pluriversal Learning: Pathways Toward a World of Many Worlds," *Nordia Geographical Publications* 47(5), 2019: 85–109; B. Rodríguez-Labajosa, I. Yánez, P. Bond, L. Greyle, S. Munguti, G. Uyi Ojo, and W. Overbeek, "Not So Natural an Alliance? Degrowth and Environmental Justice Movements in the Global South," *Ecological Economics* 157, 2019: 175–84.

18 J.F. Gerber and R. Rajeswari, "Post-Growth in the Global South? Some Reflections from India and Bhutan," *Ecological Economics* 150, 2018: 353–8; R. Verma, "Gross National Happiness: Meaning, Measure and Degrowth in a Living Development

Alternative," *Journal of Political Ecology* 24(1), 2017: 476–90.

19 A. Cox Hall, "Neo-Monastics in North Carolina, De-Growth and a Theology of Enough," *Journal of Political Ecology* 24(1), 2017: 543–65.

20 A. Beling and J. Vanhulst, *Desarrollo non sancto: La religion como actor emergente en el debate global sobre el futuro del planeta*, Mexico City: Siglo XXI Editores México, 2019.

21 K. Polanyi, *The Great Transformation*, New York: Farrar & Rinehart, 1944.

22 United Nations Population Division, Household Size & Composition, 2018: United States of America (2019), at https://population.un.org/Household/ind ex.html#/countries/840.

2 Sacrifices of Growth

1 W. Steffen et al., "Planetary Boundaries: Guiding Human Development on a Changing Planet," *Science* 347(6223), 2015: 1259855-1–10.

2 D. Harvey, *Marx, Capital and the Madness of Economic Reason*, New York: Oxford University Press, 2018.

3 R. Seaford, *Money and the Early Greek Mind: Homer, Philosophy, Tragedy*, Cambridge: Cambridge University Press, 2004.

4 M. Schmelzer, *The Hegemony of Growth: The OECD and the Making of the Economic Growth Paradigm*, Cambridge: Cambridge University Press, 2016, p. 164.

5 D. Harvey, *A Brief History of Neoliberalism*, New York: Oxford University Press, 2007.

6 D. DeSilver, "For Most US Workers, Real Wages Have Barely Budged in Decades," Pew Research Center, August 7, 2018, at https://www.pewresearch.org/fact-tank/2018/08/07/for-most-us-workers-real-wages-have-barely-budged-for-decades.

7 J. Schor, *The Overworked American: The Unexpected Decline of Leisure*, New York: Basic Books, 1992.

8 L. Berger, J.M. Collins, and L. Cuesta, "Household Debt and Adult Depressive Symptoms in the United States," *Journal of Family and Economic Issues* 37(1), 2015: 42–57.

9 G. Gheorghe, "World Debt Hits Record High of USD 247 Trillion in Q1," *Business Review*, July 11, 2018, at http://business-review.eu/money/world-debt-hits-record-high-of-usd-247-trillion-in-q1–176496.

10 L. Elliot, "Debt Crisis Warning as Poorest Countries' Repayment Bills Soar," *Guardian*, April 3, 2019, at https://www.theguardian.com/business/2019/apr/03/debt-crisis-warning-as-poorest-countries-repayment-bills-soar.

11 K. Aiginger, "Why Growth Performance Differed Across Countries in the Recent Crisis: The Impact of Pre-Crisis Conditions," *Review of Economics & Finance* 1 (2011): 35–52.

12 P. Wargan, "A Green New Deal for Europe," *Tribune*, May 14, 2019, at https://tribunemag.co.uk/2019/05/a-green-new-deal-for-europe.

13 S. Sassen, "Who Owns Our Cities – and Why This Urban Takeover Should Concern Us All," *Guardian*,

November 24, 2015, at https://www.theguardian. com/cities/2015/nov/24/who-owns-our-cities-and-why-this-urban-takeover-should-concern-us-all.

14 P. Crerar and J. Prynn, "Revealed: How Foreign Buyers Have Bought 100 bn of London Property in Six Years," *Evening Standard*, October 21, 2015, at https://www.standard.co.uk/news/london/revealed-how-foreign-buyers-have-bought-100bn-of-london-property-in-six-years-a3095936.html.

15 B. Gilbert, "People are Pooping More Than Ever on the Streets of San Francisco," *Business Insider*, April 18, 2019, at https://www.businessinsider.es/san-francisco-human-poop-problem-2019–4?r=US&IR=T.

16 United Nations Human Rights: Office of the High Commissioner, Statement on Visit to the United Kingdom, by Professor Philip Alston, United Nations Rapporteur on extreme poverty and human rights (2018), at https://www.ohchr.org/EN/NewsEvents/Pages/DisplayNews.aspx?NewsID=23881&LangID=E.

17 M. Karanikolos, P. Mladovsky, J. Cylus, S. Thomson, S. Basu, D. Stuckler, J. Mackenbach, and M. McKee, "Financial Crisis, Austerity, and Health in Europe," *The Lancet* 381(9874), 2013: 1323–31.

18 M. Lang, "A Historical Victory in Ecuador," *Radical Ecological Democracy*, October 19, 2019, at https://www.radicalecologicaldemocracy.org/historical-victory-in-ecuador.

19 "France's Bird Population Collapses Due to Pesticides," Desdemona Despair, March 22, 2018, at

https://desdemonadespair.net/2018/03/frances-bird-population-collapses-due.html.

20 J. Ellis, "The Honey Bee Crisis," *Outlooks on Pest Management* 23(1), 2012: 35–40.

21 United Nations Report, "Nature's Dangerous Decline 'Unprecedented'; Species Extinction Rates 'Accelerating'" (2019), at https://www.un.org/sus tainabledevelopment/blog/2019/05/nature-decline-unprecedented-report.

22 J. Vidal, "'Tip of the Iceberg': Is our Destruction of Nature Responsible for Covid-19?," *Guardian*, 18 March 2020, at https://www.theguardian.com/environment/2020/mar/18/tip-of-the-iceberg-is-our-destruction-of-nature-responsible-for-covid-19-aoe; R. Wallace, *Big Farms Make Big Flu: Dispatches on Influenza, Agribusiness, and the Nature of Science*, New York: NYU Press, 2016.

23 F. Mathuros, "More Plastic than Fish in the Ocean by 2050: Report Offers Blueprint for Change," World Economic Forum, January 19, 2016, at https://www. weforum.org/press/2016/01/more-plastic-than-fish-in-the-ocean-by-2050-report-offers-blueprint-for-change.

24 Y. Robiou du Pont and M. Meinshausen, "Warming Assessment of the Bottom-up Paris Agreement Emissions Pledges," *Nature Communications* 9, 2018.

25 P.J. Burke, M. Shahiduzzaman, and D.I. Stern, "Carbon Dioxide Emissions in the Short Run: The Rate and Sources of Economic Growth Matter," *Global Environmental Change* 33, 2015: 109–21.

26 S. Beckert, *Empire of Cotton: A Global History*, New York: Vintage, 2015.

27 S. Federici, *Caliban and the Witch: Women, the Body and Primitive Accumulation*, Chico, CA: AK Press, 2004.

28 S. Paulson, *Masculinities and Feminities in Latin America's Uneven Development*, New York: Routledge, 2015.

29 Cited in A. Escobar, *Encountering Development*, Princeton: Princeton University Press, 2011, p. 3.

3 Making Changes on the Ground

1 D. Bollier, "Commoning as a Transformative Social Paradigm" (2016), at http://www.bollier.org/blog/commoning-transformative-social-paradigm.

2 L. Gezon and S. Paulson (eds.), "Degrowth, Culture and Power," Special Section of 15 articles, *Journal of Political Ecology* 24, 2017.

3 Environmental Justice Atlas, at https://ejatlas.org.

4 J. Otto, "Finding Common Ground: Exploring Synergies between Degrowth and Environmental Justice in Chiapas, Mexico," *Journal of Political Ecology* 24(1), 2017: 491–503.

5 P. Goodman, "The City That Cycles With the Young, the Old, the Busy and the Dead," *New York Times*, November 9, 2019, at https://www.nytimes.com/2019/11/09/world/europe/biking-copenhagen.html.

6 A. Varvarousis, "Crisis, Liminality and the Decolonization of the Social Imaginary,"

Environment and Planning E: Nature and Space 2(3), 2019: 493–512.

7 G. Monbiot, "The Horror Films Got it Wrong: This Virus has Turned Us into Caring Neighbours," *Guardian*, 31 March 2020, at https://www.theguardi an.com/commentisfree/2020/mar/31/virus-neighbou rs-covid-19.

8 G.A. García López, "Performing Counter-Hegemonic Common(s) Senses: Rearticulating Democracy, Community and Forests in Puerto Rico," *Capitalism Nature Socialism* 28(3), 2017: 88–107.

9 J.K. Gibson-Graham, "Diverse Economies: Performative Practices for 'Other Worlds'," *Progress in Human Geography* 32(5), 2008: 613–32.

10 L. Benería, G. Berik, and M. Floro, *Gender, Development and Globalization: Economics as if All People Mattered*, Abingdon: Routledge, 2015.

11 J. Conill, M. Castells, A. Cardenas, and L. Servon, "Beyond the Crisis: The Emergence of Alternative Economic Practices," in *Aftermath: The Cultures of the Economic Crisis*, Oxford: Oxford University Press, 2012, pp. 210–50.

12 G. Dafermos, "The Catalan Integral Cooperative, P2P Foundation," at http://p2pfoundation.net/wp-content/uploads/2017/10/The-Catalan-Integral-Co operative.pdf.

13 Xarxa d'economia solidária de Catalunya, Informe del mercat social (2018), at http://mercatsocial.xes. cat/wp-content/uploads/sites/2/2016/04/informe-mer catsocial-2018_final.pdf.

14 A. Leach, "Happy Together: Lonely Baby Boomers

Turn to Co-housing," *Guardian*, August 15, 2018, at https://www.theguardian.com/world/2018/aug/15/happy-together-lonely-baby-boomers-turn-to-co-housing.

15 M. Altieri and V. Toledo, "The Agroecological Revolution in Latin America: Rescuing Nature, Ensuring Food Sovereignty and Empowering Peasants," *Journal of Peasant Studies* 38(3), 2011: 587–612.

16 E. McGuirk, "Timebanking in New Zealand as a Prefigurative Strategy Within a Wider Degrowth Movement," *Journal of Political Ecology* 24(1), 2017: 595–609.

17 V. Kostakis and A. Roos, "New Technologies Won't Reduce Scarcity, But Here's Something That Might," *Harvard Business Review*, June 1, 2018, at https://hbr.org/2018/06/new-technologies-wont-reduce-scarcity-but-heres-something-that-might.

4 Path-Breaking Reforms

1 House Resolution, 116th Congress, 1st Session, at https://www.congress.gov/bill/116th-congress/house-resolution/109/text.

2 D. Adler and P. Wargan, "10 Pillars of the New Green Deal for Europe" (2019), https://www.gndforeurope.com/10-pillars-of-the-green-new-deal-for-europe.

3 A. Pettifor, *The Case for the Green New Deal*, New York: Verso Books, 2019.

4 UCL Institute for Global Prosperity, "IGP's Social

Prosperity Network Publishes the UK's First Report on Universal Basic Services" (2017), at https://www.ucl.ac.uk/bartlett/igp/news/2017/oct/igps-social-prosperity-network-publishes-uks-first-report-universal-basic-services.

5 J. Arcarons, D. Raventós, and L. Torrens, "Una Propuesta de Financiación de una Renta Básica Universal en Plena Crisis Económica," *Sin Permiso* III, Monografico Renta Basica, 2013.

6 L. Haagh, *The Case for Universal Basic Income*, Cambridge: Polity Press, 2019.

7 K. Widerquist, *A Critical Analysis of Basic Income Experiments for Researchers, Policymakers, and Citizens*, London: Palgrave, 2018.

8 D. Raventós, *Basic Income: The Material Conditions of Freedom*, London: Pluto Press, 2007.

9 M. Lawhon and T. McCreary, "Beyond Jobs vs Environment: On the Potential of Universal Basic Income to Reconfigure Environmental Politics," *Antipode* 52(2), 2020: 452–74.

10 G. D'Alisa and C. Cattaneo, "Household Work and Energy Consumption: A Degrowth Perspective: Catalonia's Case Study," *Journal of Cleaner Production* 38, 2012: 71–9.

11 M. Bausells, "Superblocks to the Rescue: Barcelona's Plan to Give Streets Back to Residents," *Guardian*, May 17, 2016, at https://www.theguardian.com/cities/2016/may/17/superblocks-rescue-barcelona-spain-plan-give-streets-back-residents.

12 Xarxa d'economia solidária de Catalunya (XES), "15 mesures cap a l'Economia Social i Solidária als

municipis," at http://xes.cat/wp-content/uploads/2019/04/15mesures_2019.pdf.

13 N. Ashford and G. Kallis, "A Four-Day Workweek: A Policy for Improving Employment and Environmental Conditions in Europe," *European Financial Review*, April–May 2013: 53–8.

14 Federal Motor Carrier Safety Administration (FMCSA), Summary of Hours of Service Regulations (2017), at https://www.fmcsa.dot.gov/regulations/hours-service/summary-hours-service-regulations.

15 K.W. Knight, E.A. Rosa, and J.B. Schor, "Could Working Less Reduce Pressures on the Environment? A Cross-National Panel Analysis of OECD Countries, 1970–2007," *Global Environmental Change* 23(4), 2013: 691–700.

16 J. Boyce, *The Case for Carbon Dividends*, Cambridge: Polity Press, 2019.

17 D. Roberts, "The 5 Most Important Questions About Carbon Taxes, Answered" (2019), Vox, at https://www.vox.com/energy-and-environment/2018/7/20/17584376/carbon-tax-congress-republicans-cost-economy.

18 Office of the Under Secretary of Defense, National Defense Budget Estimates for FY 2020, at https://comptroller.defense.gov/Portals/45/Documents/defbudget/fy2020/FY20_Green_Book.pdf.

19 T. Piketty, *Capital in the 21st Century*, Cambridge, MA: The Belknap Press of Harvard University Press, 2014; E. Saez and G. Zucman, *The Triumph of Injustice: How the Rich Dodge Taxes and How to Make Them Pay*, New York: W.W. Norton & Company, 2019.

20 Tax Policy Center, Urban Institute & Brookings Institution, "Historical Highest Marginal Income Tax Rates" (2018), at https://www.taxpolicycenter.org/statistics/historical-highest-marginal-income-tax-rates.

21 J. Stiglitz and M. Pieth, "Overcoming the Shadow Economy," *International Policy Analysis*, November 2016, at https://library.fes.de/pdf-files/iez/12922.pdf.

22 S. Pizzigati, *The Case for a Maximum Wage*, Cambridge: Polity Press, 2018.

23 See https://www.wagemark.org.

24 G. Morgenson, "Portland Adopts Surtax on C.E.O. Pay to Fight Income Gap," *New York Times*, December 7, 2016, at https://www.nytimes.com/2016/12/07/business/economy/portland-oregon-tax-executive-pay.html.

25 A. Hornborg, "How to Turn an Ocean Liner: A Proposal for Voluntary Degrowth by Redesigning Money for Sustainability, Justice, and Resilience," *Journal of Political Ecology* 24(1), 2017; Positive Money, "Escaping Growth Dependency" (2018), at https://positivemoney.org/publications/escaping-growth-dependency.

26 J. Hickel, "Aid in Reverse: How Poor Countries Develop Rich Countries," *Guardian*, January 14, 2017, at https://www.theguardian.com/global-development-professionals-network/2017/jan/14/aid-in-reverse-how-poor-countries-develop-rich-countries.

27 J. Martínez-Alier, "Ecological Debt and Property Rights on Carbon Sinks and Reservoirs," *Capitalism Nature Socialism* 13(1), 2010: 115–19.

5 Strategies for Mobilization

1 E.O. Wright, *Envisioning Real Utopias*, New York: Verso Books, 2010.

2 D. Noonan, "The 25% Revolution – How Big Does a Minority Have to Be to Reshape Society?" *The Scientific American*, June 8, 2018, at https://www.scientificamerican.com/article/the-25-revolution-how-big-does-a-minority-have-to-be-to-reshape-society.

3 M. Taylor, "Majority of UK Public Back 2030 Zero-Carbon Target – Poll," *Guardian*, November 7, 2019, at https://www.theguardian.com/environment/2019/nov/07/majority-of-uk-public-back-2030-zero-carbon-target-poll?CMP=Share_iOSApp_Other.

4 J. Elks, "Havas: 'Smarter' Consumers Will Significantly Alter Economic Models and the Role of Brands" (2014), Sustainable Brands, at https://sustainablebrands.com/read/defining-the-next-economy/havas-smarter-consumers-will-significantly-alter-economic-models-and-the-role-of-brands.

5 F. Demaria, "When Degrowth Enters the Parliament," Ecologist, January 16, 2017, at https://theecologist.org/2017/jan/16/when-degrowth-enters-parliament.

6 S. Samuel, "Forget GDP – New Zealand is Prioritizing Gross National Well-Being," Vox, June 8, 2019, at https://www.vox.com/future-perfect/2019/6/8/18656710/new-zealand-wellbeing-budget-bhutan-happiness.

7 K. Aronoff, "Is Nationalization an Answer to Climate Change?" The Intercept, September 8, 2018,

143

at https://theintercept.com/2018/09/08/jeremy-corb
yn-labour-climate-change.

8 J. Gray, *Gray's Anatomy: Selected Writings*, London:
Penguin Books, 2010, p. 127.

9 J. Gray, "Why the Greens Should Stop Playing God,"
UnHerd, June 3, 2019, at https://unherd.com/2019/
06/climate-change-and-the-extinction-of-thought.

10 D. Harvey, "Why Marx's Capital Still Matters,"
Jacobin, July 12, 2018, at https://www.jacobinmag.
com/2018/07/karl-marx-capital-david-harvey

11 J. Chan and J. Curnow, "Taking Up Space: Men,
Masculinity, and the Student Climate Movement,"
RCC Perspectives 4, 2017: 77–85.

12 C. Dengler and L.M. Seebacher, "What About
the Global South? Towards a Feminist Decolonial
Degrowth Approach," *Ecological Economics* 157,
2019: 247.

13 A. Escobar, "Degrowth, Postdevelopment, and
Transitions: A Preliminary Conversation,"
Sustainability Science 10(3), 2015: 451.

14 A. Beling, J. Vanhulst, F. Demaria, V. Rabi,
A. Carballo, and J. Pelen, "Discursive Synergies for
a 'Great Transformation' Towards Sustainability:
Pragmatic Contributions to a Necessary Dialogue
Between Human Development, Degrowth, and Buen
Vivir," *Ecological Economics* (144), 2017: 304–13.

15 B. Rodríguez-Labajos, I. Yánez, P. Bond, L. Greyle,
S. Munguti, G. Uyi Ojo, and W. Overbeek, "Not So
Natural an Alliance? Degrowth and Environmental
Justice Movements in the Global South," *Ecological
Economics* 157, 2019: 176.

16 S. Paulson, "Pluriversal Learning: Pathways Toward a World of Many Worlds," *Nordia Geographical Publications* 47(5), 2019: 85–109.

17 See the Global Tapestry of Alternatives (GTA): https://globaltapestryofalternatives.org.

18 M.E. Mann, "Radical Reform and the Green New Deal," *Nature* 573, 2019: 340–1, at https://www.nature.com/articles/d41586–019–02738–7.

19 P. Nirmal and D. Rocheleau, "Decolonizing Degrowth in the Post-Development Convergence: Questions, Experiences, and Proposals from Two Indigenous Territories," *Nature and Space* 2(3), 2019: 465–92.

Frequently Asked Questions

1 D. Stern, "The Rise and Fall of the Environmental Kuznets Curve," *World Development* 32(8), 2004: 1419–39.

2 For data and further references see J. Hickel and G. Kallis, "Is Green Growth Possible?" *New Political Economy*, 2019, doi: 10.1080/13563467.2019.1598964.

3 J.K. Steinberger, F. Krausmann, M. Getzner, H. Schandl, and J. West, "Development and Dematerialization: An International Study," *PLOS ONE* 8(10), 2013: e70385.

4 T.O. Wiedmann, H. Schandl, M. Lenzen, D. Moran, D., S. Suh, J. West, and K. Kanemoto, "The Material Footprint of Nations," *Proceedings of the National Academy of Sciences* 112(20), 2015: 6271–6.

5 Hickel and Kallis, "Is Green Growth Possible?"

6 B. Alcott, M. Giampietro, K. Mayumi, and J. Polimeni, *The Jevons Paradox and the Myth of Resource Efficiency Improvements*, Abingdon: Routledge, 2012.

7 T. Murphy, "Can Economic Growth Last?" Do the Math blog, July 14, 2011, at https://dothemath.ucsd.edu/2011/07/can-economic-growth-last.

8 W.L. Rees, "Don't Call Me a Pessimist on Climate Change. I Am a Realist," The Tyee, November 11, 2019, at https://thetyee.ca/Analysis/2019/11/11/Climate-Change-Realist-Face-Facts.

9 R. York, "Do Alternative Energy Sources Displace Fossil Fuels?" *Nature Climate Change* 2, 2012: 441–3.

10 See A. Vatn and D.W. Bromley, "Choices without Prices without Apologies," *Journal of Environmental Economics and Management* 26(2), 1994: 129–48.

11 N. Georgescu-Roegen, *The Entropy Law and the Economic Process*, Cambridge, MA: Harvard University Press, 1971.

12 M. Giampietro, "On the Circular Bioeconomy and Decoupling: Implications for Sustainable Growth," *Ecological Economics* 162, 2019: 143–56.

13 K. Anderson and A. Bows-Larkin, "Avoiding Dangerous Climate Change Demands De-Growth Strategies from Wealthier Nations" (2013), at https://kevinanderson.info/blog/avoiding-dangerous-climate-change-demands-de-growth-strategies-from-wealthier-nations.

14 C. Le Quéré et al., "Drivers of Declining CO2

Emissions in 18 Developed Economies," *Nature Climate Change* 9(3), 2019: 213–17.

15 See G. Kallis, *Degrowth*, London: Agenda Publishing, 2018, pp. 77–9.

16 P. Brown, "Cuba's Urban Farming Shows Way to Avoid Hunger," EcoWatch, November 12, 2019, at https://www.ecowatch.com/urban-farming-cuba-2641320251.html.

17 B. Lars-Arvid, L. Leuser, C. Baedeker, F. Lehmann, and S. Thomas, *Energy Sufficiency in Private Households Enabled by Adequate Appliances*, Wuppertal Institut für Klima, Umwelt, Energie, 2015, at https://epub.wupperinst.org/frontdoor/deliver/index/docId/5932/file/5932_Brischke.pdf.

18 R. Gessler and B. Volland, "On the Way to the 2000-Watt Society" (2016), at https://www.stadt-zuerich.ch/portal/en/index/portraet_der_stadt_zuerich/2000-watt_society.html.

19 M. Ravallion, "A Relative Question," *Finance & Development* 49(4), 2012: 40–3.

20 T. Piketty, *Capital in the 21st Century*, Cambridge, MA: The Belknap Press of Harvard University Press, 2014.

21 J. Steinberger, J. Roberts, G. Peters, and G. Baiocchi, "Pathways of Human Development and Carbon Emissions Embodied in Trade," *Nature Climate Change* 2, 2012: 81–5.

22 W.F. Lamb and N.D. Rao, "Human Development in a Climate-Constrained World: What the Past Says About the Future," *Global Environmental Change* 33, 2015: 14–22.

23 Positive Money, "Escaping Growth Dependency" (2018), at https://positivemoney.org/publications/escaping-growth-dependency.

24 Kallis, *Degrowth*, pp. 109–10.

25 For a more detailed discussion of population, immigration, and degrowth, see Kallis, *Degrowth*, pp. 180–7.

26 For more detailed data, debates, and references see Kallis, *Degrowth*, pp. 87–95.

27 If you want to get closer to the degrowth community you are welcome to join our summer schools (https://summerschool.degrowth.org) or master program (https://master.degrowth.org), the biennial international degrowth conferences (https://www.degrowth.info/en/conferences), the Feminisms and Degrowth Alliance (FaDA – https://www.degrowth.info/en/2017/02/feminisms-and-degrowth-alliance-fada-newly-launched), or the Global Tapestry of Alternatives (https://globaltapestryofalternatives.org).

Index

Index

Index